Contents

Dedication

This book is dedicated
    to the magnificent wise person inside of you
    to the beauty in and around you
    to the love and joy flowing to and from you
    and to the celebration of life within you.

Acknowledgements

Thank you to the teens who freely shared your concerns with us. Special thanks to Lauren, Nik, and Kelsea for their opinions, advice, and support, and to Mike, Debby, and Bob for their love and encouragement.

Over the years and through various editions we've had terrific input from the staff and students at San Luis Obispo Senior High School, Monterey Road School, Atascadero Junior High, and Atascadero High School. They've all been wonderfully helpful and open.

Sharon and Cindi put forth tremendous creativity and talent on previous editions and we've been so grateful to have that continue with Gayle, Katy, and Melissa W. on this edition.

Finally, thanks so much to Jean and Cheyenne at Impact for all of their patience and effort!

Introduction

Remember when you asked a teacher how to spell a word and she told you, "Look it up in the dictionary." Didn't you wonder, "How can I look it up in the dictionary if I don't know how to spell it?!"

Life's a lot like that when you're a teenager: "You can't get a job without experience." "So," you wonder, "how can I get experience without a job?" It's not always easy. There will always be choices to make and often obstacles in your way...

That's how the first two editions of *Teen Esteem* began, and life certainly hasn't gotten any easier since we first wrote those words! Nik, an eighteen-year-old friend of mine, recently told me, "It's even worse than that, really. It's more like I don't even know what *word* I'm supposed to be looking up, and have no idea where to find a dictionary!"

It's certainly a lot easier to figure out where you're going if you know where — and *who* — you are, though. Knowing yourself gives you the self-confidence you need to make good choices and overcome tough obstacles. But how can you get to know yourself until you've had a chance to make your *own* choices and overcome your *own* obstacles? (How can you look it up until you know how to spell it..., or at least until you know what the word is?!)

It's tougher than ever to be a teen. (The teen years have always been tough, of course.) You're in your first "middle age" — in the middle between childhood and adulthood. Nobody — including you — can say exactly when it's right to consider you a "child" (don't you hate that word now?) and when to consider you an "adult."

Your parents are saying "DON'T" a lot, as you test the limits they want to place on your activities. They care very much about you, and they want to protect you as long as they can. They also know that you're growing up fast, and they have to let go, but that's a tough thing for parents to do after twelve or fifteen years of being the most important people in your life. You may feel as though you are very different from your parents right now, and that you might decide to develop your own goals or find a unique direction for your life: you want to become *yourself*.

Your friends or classmates are saying "DO" most of the time: "Do stay out late," "Do smoke," "Do drink," "Do drugs," "Do try sex," "DO IT." And it is important to have friends, and to "fit in" with your group — only natural to want to be like them, but you want to become *yourself*.

TV, music, movies, the Internet, and other media are shouting their own messages in your direction: "Just do it," "If it doesn't get all over the place, it doesn't belong in your face."

You'd like to follow some of those media suggestions, too, but you want to become *yourself*.

Everybody seems to have a plan for how you should live your life. So how do you get to be *yourself*?

This book has some ideas about self-direction, ways to help you sort *yourself* out from all these forces competing for your loyalty.

We'll talk about: *who you are; who you want to be (and who you want to become)*, and *how you get there*. We'll also discuss your goals, your rights, ways to say "no," respecting yourself, taking care of yourself, standing up for yourself (and for what's important to you), asking for what *you* want, and lots more.

We don't have all the answers, but we'd like to help you build some of the skills and attitudes you need so you can become the person you want to be.

We wrote this book to help you feel good enough about yourself to try to get what *you* want out of life. That's not being selfish —

it's what we all need in order to be happy: *self-esteem*. Or, in your case *TEEN ESTEEM*.

If you're reading this book because somebody told you to — maybe a parent or a teacher — you're probably not too excited about it. But hold on a minute. Give us a chance to surprise you.

This book isn't going to tell you what you *should* want or what you *should* do to be happy. We *will* talk about things you can do to be happy with who you are and where you're going. We think it's O.K. to like yourself, to stand up for yourself, and to take charge of your life.

You may decide to work hard, to set a goal and really go for it. Or you may want to take it easy and just get by. Anything is possible — you have lots of choices.

Those maps in shopping malls that say "You are here" are there for a reason: it's a lot easier to know where you're going — and how to get there — if you know where you are now. This book might just give you a better idea where you are, and help you build the skills you need to get where you want to be.

Chapter 1

What Do You Want from Life?
(Your Goals)

You've been setting goals since you were little.

When you were somewhere around a year old, you probably started to climb, and you decided to make it up onto the couch, the chairs, the coffee table, the dining room table, the sink, the refrigerator.... Later, you saw someone do a somersault, and figured, "I can do that." At three or five or seven, you began learning to read by deciding it was worth your while. About that same time, you fell off a bike lots of times before your persistent effort to reach that goal helped you master the tricky balance, and brought success.

More recently, you might have decided to make the team (was it basketball, marching band, track, livestock judging, debate, forensics, gymnastics, football, soccer, yearbook staff,...?). Maybe your goals have been more personal (winning an art competition, asking out that special person, getting your story published, acing a class, mastering a new game or computer program, playing the keyboard,...?).

Whatever the field, whatever your style, you've been setting goals for yourself all your life. And you've achieved some of them too. Maybe you didn't star in tennis, but you made the team. Your scores may not have won the online tournament, but you had a lot of fun competing. And along the way, you've learned a lot about setting goals for yourself.

As you get older, of course, the goals become more important. Now you're deciding about *habits* which may last a lifetime (music, reading, studying, smoking, drinking, exercise, drugs, . . .), about the *direction* of your life (college, military service, jobs, marriage, . . .), about your *values* (political, religious, social, ethical, . . .).

What Do You Stand For?

To take charge of your life you have to get to know what's important to you. How can you make decisions for yourself if you don't know what you *stand for*?

What do you believe in? What are your feelings and opinions about:

Money	War and peace
Religion	Gun control
Politics	Drug use
The death penalty	Education
Green Movement, global warming	Sex

What Do You Need?

We all have lots of needs: food, sleep, a place to live, money. We also need to be loved, to be touched, to have friends, to have approval, to be accepted.

By knowing what you need and being willing to take care of your own needs, you won't be dependent on others to meet these needs. You gain independence and self-reliance by counting on and caring for yourself. Caring for and loving yourself means that you're free to choose to care for another — you're not desperate to find love or approval, you aren't willing to do *anything* to win it, and you won't give up your own values to keep it. People who give up being themselves to win approval from others become slaves

Getting to Know You

- *Important Things*

   Write down the 5 most important things in your life. Number them from 1 to 5 in order of their importance to you. Share with a friend or a classmate how you feel about the things on this list.

- *Looking Forward*

   Your list of the 5 most important things in your life may change as you grow older. Imagine what your list might look like in 10 years, 30 years.

- *Looking Back*

   Imagine that you are 95 years old. You are peacefully sitting on a porch looking out over a beautiful scene... mountains, rolling hills, grasslands, a lake. Now let your mind go over your life. What are the important things you have done? Have you accomplished what you set out to do? Do you have children and grandchildren? Who are your friends? What fun did you have? Did you have adventures? Loves? Was it a good life? Are you happy with yourself? Did you give something back to the world? Write down some of the things you discover from this "imaging." How would you like to plan your life so that at 95 you feel satisfied?

to it. The sad part is that they often lose the attention and approval they are trying so hard for anyway because they've given up the unique qualities that make them lovable! You need not be a slave to approval if you know how to love yourself.

If you are willing to treat yourself well ... keep yourself healthy, attractive, and happy... then other people will want to be your friends. If you try to hold onto people by being helpless, clingy or sick, they may eventually tire of your neediness and move on to someone who can support them, too — possibly after taking advantage of you. Being dependent and needy may attract some people to you, but it does not create healthy relationships.

Your Goals: If You Know Where You Are Going, You Are More Likely to Get There

Having a plan, either a life plan or a plan of action for your immediate future, will help you feel there is a direction to your life.

It's easy to drift through life, doing what others do or doing what other people expect you to do — but what are your goals for yourself? Write them down. A 1-year plan, a 5-year plan, a 10-year plan, even 20-, 30-, 40-year plans. Where do you want to be? What do you want to be doing? If it is hard for you to imagine, then try daydreaming. Fantasizing and daydreaming help you try out as many kinds of life plans as you wish. Have fun imagining yourself in lots of different kinds of life styles. See what feels good, looks like fun, fits your personality, goals, beliefs, moods.

Goal!

- Identifying who you are now — what you believe in, what you stand for — will help you figure out where you are going and who you want to be.

- Make a list of your goals for the day, the week, the month, the year. Change them as needed. Celebrate each achievement.

- Be aware of your human needs. Take care to meet them. Make a list of the things you need to be happy, and work to meet your own needs.

Chapter 2

Your Right to Be Yourself
(Your Rights)

"It's a free country."

Sure, we say it a lot in the United States, but it doesn't mean that there aren't any limits on how we live. We obey limits every day — often without even thinking about them. Most of us:

- drive our cars on the right side of the road and stop at red lights.
- leave a store when the clerk says it's closing time.
- go to the end of a line at a fast-food restaurant, movie theater, or concert.
- do what the coach tells us to do at practices and in games.
- and more . . .

You can choose not to obey these limits — but you may:

- get your license taken away.
- be arrested for trespassing.
- be kicked out of a restaurant, a theater, or a concert.
- be cut from the team.

Driving a car is a privilege that the Department of Motor Vehicles offers. Being on the soccer (debate, swim, robotics, hockey) team is a privilege that your parents and school might allow. You can earn more privileges by accepting more responsibilities, but while you're a teenager your parents or guardians have the final say.

At times you've probably wondered if you have any rights at all!

Just because you live in a democracy doesn't mean you feel free. As a child you were told what to do constantly. But as you grow older, you are given more chance to take charge of your life. You probably have some restrictions on your activities, such as how much money you have to spend, how late you can stay out, how long you can talk on the phone, where you go and with whom. It won't be long before you'll be making all the decisions in your life — not just the day-to-day stuff, but what you believe in: your values, rights, needs and goals.

Sure, you probably can't wait . . . but are you *sure* you're ready?

Knowing your rights helps you make decisions and stand up for yourself — it frees you from other people's put downs and manipulations because it is more difficult for them to convince you to do something you don't want or need to do. Here is a list of ten of the human rights that we like and take for ourselves. You may add your own rights to this list and, of course, ignore the ones that don't fit you.

I claim the right . . .

1. to be treated with respect.
2. to have my own feelings and express them.
3. to have my own opinions and express them.
4. to be listened to and taken seriously.
5. to decide what is important to me.
6. to ask for what I want (others have the right to refuse).
7. to make mistakes, and to learn from them.
8. to control my own body.
9. to have some privacy or space of my own.
10. to take responsibility for my own choices, behavior, thoughts and feelings.

Number 10 is the "biggie." It means that you take control of your life by acting the way you choose *and being willing to take the consequences*. The way *other* people want you to act and think becomes less important.

Here's an exercise that may make this business of "rights" more real to you:

Pick one of those rights which feels important to you. Sit quietly and imagine it entering your body and mind. Inhale the sentence. Breathe it in until you feel it in every cell of your body. Accept it as belonging to you. Now you can begin to live by it as you go through each day. You have made it part of you. Do that with each right that you want to give yourself. If you have a hard time imagining it entering your body, then say it to yourself or write it down several times a day. When you find yourself thinking, "That's it! All right! Yeah!" then you know you have it.

For example, let's say you decide to claim for yourself the right to be listened to and taken seriously.

What would that mean to you? Who would be listening? (Friends? Parents? Classmates? People on the street? Pushy sales clerks?) How would your life be different? (People will listen? They'll do what you ask?) What will you be saying that you haven't said before? (Answering questions in class? Telling rude and manipulative people to take off? Expressing opinions about music?) How will you feel? (Stronger? Anxious? Foolish? Powerful?) How will you make it a part of your everyday life? (Practice at home? Tell all your friends? Speak out in class once a day?)

When you have given yourself a right:

- **There will be a change in you.** People might not know why, but they'll treat you differently, with more respect. Your body language will express your new rights — you won't feel (or look) like a pushover.

- **It will be hard for people to manipulate you.** For instance, you may claim the right to make mistakes. When someone points out a mistake, you can smile and say, "Yeah, I sure blew that one," or "I'm only human, you know?" or just, "You're right." Instead of feeling guilty, making excuses, getting defensive or denying it, remember it's all right to "mess up" — you are still a good person.

- **You will have given yourself freedom of choice.** Instead of becoming an engineer you can become a nurse, or vice versa. Instead of getting married, you can travel around the world. Instead of doing the same thing every day, you can vary your routine. *You* are the only one who knows what is right for you. Your mother may want you to become a doctor and your father may want you to go into business. (They may want you to do these things because they didn't get the chance to do them themselves or because it is traditional in your family.) You are the only one who can decide what you want to be. You need to be true to yourself.

You grow by learning how to take care of yourself. Making decisions for yourself — even wrong decisions — helps you learn. Your parents and friends can give you chances to grow, learn, and feel more competent by acknowledging your rights.

Many schools have students' rights and responsibilities written out. Because democracy is based on basic human rights for all, it is important that you become aware of your rights and not allow people, organizations or government institutions to take them away. Freedom is based on these rights; the Constitution guarantees them to us.

Claim for yourself the rights you want. Others will respect you for it. When you know your rights, you can stand up for them, be guided by them, and make decisions more easily. Knowing your rights helps you set your own goals and achieve them.

That's Right!

Knowing your rights helps you take control of your life and make the best decisions that you can for *you*.

- Practice giving yourself the rights you want. How will you act? How will your life change?

- Practice respecting others' rights. How can you do this?

- When you hear people complaining, ask them what they plan to DO about the bad situation...instead of "helping" them or just listening (though there is a time and place for that too, and we will discuss more about listening in chapter 6).

- Re-read the Bill of Rights — the first ten amendments to the U.S. Constitution. How do those rights compare with your personal "Bill of Rights"? (Ask a teacher or librarian if you need help finding a copy of this.)

Chapter 3

R-E-S-P-E-C-T
(Liking Yourself)

How do you like you?

If you like yourself, you expect good things to happen to you. Liking yourself doesn't mean that you think you're perfect — or that you like the faults you have. You can accept your faults and still hope to change or improve. To like yourself you start by accepting who you are.

So we begin by trying to convince you that you're great and deserve a good life. Learn to think and talk about yourself in positive ways. When you think of yourself as a special person with gifts and talents, people treat you well. You can dream a dream, win prizes, take risks, try new things, be wonderful.

Don't laugh! It's true. You DO have special gifts and talents, even if you haven't discovered them yet! Every human being has them.

What are the qualities you look for in a friend? Someone who:

- is a good listener?
- tries to cheer you up when you are down?
- makes you laugh?
- shows you she cares?

You can do all of these things for yourself. And the good news is that learning to treat yourself this way will also help you learn to be a better friend to others!

Too many people focus on what they *don't* have instead of the wonderful things they *do* have. Listen to yourself. Do you put yourself down more than anyone else? Do you call yourself dumb, fat, clumsy, ugly? If so, it's time to shape up the conversation that goes on inside you. Stop being rude to yourself! Your own put-downs are the worst *enemy*.

Treat yourself with RESPECT. Believe you are a great person, and stand up for yourself. Be kind to yourself and you can be your own best friend.

Body Image

"I've gotta lose ten pounds."
"I want to build more muscle — I look like a wimp!"
"I wish my nose wasn't so big!"
"If I get one more zit, I'm not going to school!"

People talk about their bodies all the time — and usually what they say isn't very nice! Not many people seem to be happy with the bodies they have. After all, every day we see gorgeous models, actors, and actresses — on TV, in magazines, in movies, on the Internet. They're beautiful — nearly perfect. Of course they are: they've paid to have their teeth capped or whitened, their hair and makeup professionally done, their clothes custom-designed or fitted; they may have personal trainers to help them shape their

"Jennifer's" Story

It got to be so easy. It was something I was really good at — that all my friends had such a hard time with. At first they said, "Oh my God, you're getting so skinny! I hate you! What do you wear now, anyway? A size zero??" And I loved it! I'd always been bigger than all my friends. But I didn't want to stop losing weight, I mean, what if it came back? So I started to get really scared to eat anything, thinking that I'd get too fat if I did. I'd let myself have maybe three grapes and an apple all day long, and then I'd go for a run and come home and do sit-ups and stuff. And everyday I'd look in the mirror and still think I was too fat.

My mom was bugging me all the time, telling me I was too thin and I should eat more. I'd tell her I was eating at a friend's house or something. But it didn't really matter to me what she said, because she's heavy too, and she's always saying how models are too skinny. And all the time I wanted to look just like them! I finally passed out at school and they put me in this hospital. I've been in here for weeks. They won't let me out, they won't let me run, and they've had me on an IV forever... I'm up to ninety pounds now, but they say that's still not enough for my height. I want to get out of here, but I can't make myself eat. I just don't want to turn into a cow again!

bodies, dieticians to regulate their menus, or surgery to "improve" their appearance, and — after all that — their pictures may even be altered to remove any remaining "flaws." So, how would any of us ever begin to compete?

You don't have to. You can choose to be healthy, to take care of your body, to appreciate the way it works for you. The better you feel about yourself, the more attractive you will look to others. But it's not always easy to ignore those media images, to be satisfied with your uniqueness. Your body is constantly changing. Your clothes might not fit from one day to the next. Your hair may have a mind of its own. Your voice might crack, or your skin might break out . . . You often won't be thrilled with how you look. The thing to remember is that you have something special to offer, and it's not always going to show on the outside! (See later sections in this chapter and in chapter 5 for ideas to keep yourself feeling good.)

You've heard this before, but it's true: *you will feel better about your body if you exercise regularly, stay away from drugs and alcohol, get enough sleep, and eat healthy foods* — no matter what size jeans you wear, or how big your muscles are.

Eating disorders such as anorexia nervosa, bulimia nervosa, and compulsive overeating can develop when your feelings and emotions become tied together with food. All are serious problems that can even become life-threatening. If you find yourself "obsessing" about food — thinking about eating or dieting all of the time — please talk to an adult who can help you break out of this unhealthy pattern. Or, if you think a friend may have one of these problems, encourage him or her to seek help. Eating disorders are almost impossible to fight alone.

Your Attitude

The way you think about yourself shows in your body. If you think negative thoughts, your face scowls. Your shoulders and mouth droop. You look unhappy. Life is boring, depressing, and dull. Nothing good or exciting ever happens to you. Your cup is half-empty instead of half-full.

Negative into Positive Thoughts

Your thoughts make up your attitude toward yourself. If they're negative, your life is unhappy. If they're positive, your life is happy. It's that simple. Negative thoughts are a collection of bad habits, like biting your nails or popping your gum.

It's *NOT* that tough to change habits. The hardest part is *deciding* to get rid of them. The next step is to *pay attention* to your thoughts. Then begin to *do something* about them. Here's one way: When you hear a negative thought, say "Stop." Deliberately yell (inside your head), "STOP!" Then replace that negative thought with a positive one. Here are a couple of examples:

- Negative Thought
  I have a huge, ugly nose.
  I'm too dumb to get good grades.

  STOP!

- Positive Thought
  I've got a great smile.
  I'm creative — a really good artist.

Here are some other ways to get rid of a negative thought: Pretend you're in a boat, drifting down river. Toss the negative thought overboard and watch it sink. Or see yourself relaxing in front of an open fire; stick the thought in the fire and watch it go up in flames. Or flush it down the toilet.

Of course there will be difficult times — there are in everyone's life — no one is happy *all* of the time. The key is learning to turn your focus to the positive when you can.

The Enemies Within

We all carry around with us a group of our own "enemies" — attitudes and habits which tend to rob us of self-respect. You'll probably spot some of yours in the list below. When you've identified them, start to work on getting back the respect they've stolen from you!

1. *Being Perfect.* Do you look at yourself in the mirror and say, "Gross!"? Do you consider a pimple a terminal illness? Do you hate your voice, face, body, hair, knees, feet? Is there nothing about you that's "right"? If you feel this way, you have a bad case of "the perfections."

To get rid of "the perfections," realize that you're HUMAN. Sometimes you smell, have bad breath, or sweat. Flaws are normal and natural, not fatal. Learn to love those parts of you that are different and unique. They make you YOU.

2. *Judging* (the critic within). When you judge yourself, you stop yourself from being amazing. The voice in your head says things like: "If I try to solve that problem at the board, I'll do it wrong." "If I tell the teacher I don't understand the question, everyone will think I'm stupid." (Most likely someone else in the classroom will have the same question and be thankful that you asked it!)

3. *Catastrophisizing.* "If I ask Tim for a date, he'll say no, and I'll die." Thoughts like this stop us from doing what we want. They make us into zombies, paralyzed with fear. "If I speak up in class, my voice'll crack and I'll feel like an idiot." Don't worry! Most people are too busy working on their own perfectness to bother with yours or even to notice your voice cracking.

4. *Expectations* go along with "the perfections." Let's say you're going shopping for the perfect jeans. You've got them in your mind, but you can't find them. Your day is ruined. Your whole life is pretty close to ruined. Without those jeans you won't ever look good.

Expectations can ruin a good relationship: Sarah and Matt love each other. Sarah thinks, "If Matt loved me, he'd know how to make me happy." (A crystal ball isn't given to every lover!) Sarah will never be happy with Matt until she realizes that he can't read her mind — she's got to learn to ask for what she wants.

Look at this list of expectations. How often do you do any of these?

- Expect a party to turn out just as you'd imagined.
- Expect someone to know how you like your burger done.
- Expect your friends to know how you feel without telling them.
- Expect people to act and speak the way you want them to.

- Want your mother, father, sister, brother to change, become different and "better."
- Know that there's a RIGHT way to do things (your way), and be annoyed if things don't happen your way.
- Expect people to believe the same way you do about religion, politics, drugs and sex.

If people or situations are not exactly as you expect them to be, you're upset, depressed, or angry. But YOU are the one who's feeling bad. You create unhappiness for yourself.

You don't have to go through life being unhappy and disappointed. *Just give up being judgmental and putting expectations on people and things in your life.* By letting your expectations go, you'll find a heavy burden removed. If you don't waste your energy thinking about how the party SHOULD be, then you can have a great time just being there!

5. *Blaming* is another bad habit that keeps you from enjoying life and being happy. "If Julie hadn't called me last night, I would've studied more and passed that test." You spend your life as a helpless victim when you blame. Some people spend their entire lives playing "poor me." Even when they can help themselves, they don't. (You could have told Julie you didn't have time to talk.)

6. *Living in the past and the future.* Many of us make our lives into nightmares. We collect bad things that happened to us and hug them to ourselves. "I forgot my lines in a play three years ago — and I still feel sick when I think about it." We hold on to old guilts. "I lost my best friend in the 4th grade just because I was mad and told her she was ugly." The healthy way to deal with this is to forgive yourself, learn the lesson (you learned to respect other people's feelings) and let go of the past. Move on! Anger, resentment and guilt are heavy burdens that make your life one long pain. They are in the past and no longer exist except in your mind.

Worrying is living in the future. You can scare yourself to death about what MIGHT happen ("What if I blow every catch? The team

> *Life is a journey, not a destination.*

will kill me!"). Keep track of the things you worry about. You'll find that most of them *never happen*. If you live in the future (or the past), you miss right now! You'll be happier if you just relax and enjoy life as it happens!

"But shouldn't I be planning for college, my career, my future life?" Of course you should. Just don't let your careful *planning* become needless *worrying*. There are many wonderful life experiences available every day. Enjoy at least a few of them now while you're preparing and planning for later.

Balance is the key.

Don't Miss the "Little Things" in Life

Smelling — flowers, fresh air, newly-mowed lawn, cookies baking.

Hearing — music, the wind, your heartbeat, your cat purring.

Feeling — soft clothes, wet bathing suit, warm or cool air, strong legs, feet touching the ground, standing, running.

Seeing — beauty everywhere — colors, shapes, textures, living creatures, nature, buildings, big things, little things, details.

Learning to Like Yourself

Accept yourself the way you are. Forgive those feet that turn in, or the hair that refuses to stay down or curl. Forgive yourself for having a squeaky voice. Let that pimple come and go in peace. So you're six feet tall, and you have five foot arms? Hooray for you! You are unique.

Your feelings are an important part of you too. Don't worry if you don't always feel "nice." We all have been jealous, angry, bitter, at one time or another. Allow your feelings; as long as you recognize them there is no reason to be guilty about them. After you've identified the negative feeling, you can say, "Yeah, I'm still *human!*" and then go on from there.

Your most important job in life is to *be yourself.* Believe it or not, no one expects you to be anyone else. You are already wonderful and magnificent. So why not relax and be you? Inside you is a marvelous person with skills, talents, gifts, warmth, love and caring — yes, and your share of human faults. There may be some things you'd like to change about yourself. Well, funny as it sounds, the first step toward becoming the person you want to be is to accept the person you are! If you want to become the friendliest person on campus, you must first accept yourself as someone who is not that friendly — *yet.* If you want to be a better ball player, you've got to accept your weaknesses so you'll know what you need to work on.

"Respectfully Yours"

Learning to like yourself isn't complicated. It requires a little effort to change thoughts from negative to positive. Focus on the good things in your life and think about the things you like about yourself. You'll go from a sad, grumpy person to someone who knows how to be happy and joyful. Happiness is in the present — not the future or the past.

Not every moment you experience will be happy; life occasionally throws huge challenges at us and makes it tough to find joy and escape sadness, but please learn to recognize the moments of happiness you *can* capture. This world is constantly changing: the class you don't like, the super-popular person who doesn't like *you*, the crush you can't seem to get over... they won't be in your life forever, but learning to accept and be comfortable with who you are, is a skill that can be! You can be your own best friend and learn how to love and take good care of yourself. And that's the foundation for being and doing whatever you want with your life.

Life's Like That...

Finding the good things in your life — and in yourself — and accepting your shortcomings, helps you learn to like yourself... and enjoy life more!

- Practice turning your negative thoughts into positive ones.
- Take back your self-respect from your "enemies within."
- Forgive your faults and accept yourself for who you are.

Chapter 4

What If I'm Different?
(Masks We Wear)

It's not so weird to be different. In fact most people have something about them that may seem odd to others, though they may try to hide it. We like to pretend that only certain people are different, but the truth is that we are *all* different, it's just that some people "fit in" better. Most people hide the part of themselves that is vulnerable, silly, childish, or different in order to be accepted — they act cool, adult, or make fun of other people. Some people ignore their own feelings or conscience in order to avoid being seen as "different": they might join in when their friends tease someone, or act as if a friend's behavior doesn't bother them when it does. While it's okay to have a more private self, and a public self, it is important not to change yourself so much around other people that you forget who you are. The more people start really being themselves, the more it seems that being different is something we all have in common!

Unfortunately, though, a lot of people are often frightened of new, different ideas, and can feel threatened by people they see as "other." This is sometimes called "us vs. them" thinking, where one group sees another group as less-than-human and outside their group. But even though there are people who are scared of — or even cruel to — people who are different, there are others who are open-minded and accepting of others' differences.

The New School

Ramon just moved to a new school. He missed the friends he left behind in Los Angeles. In L.A. it was not unusual to be Chicano. But in his new town, he was the only kid whose native language was Spanish, and he thought he was the only Catholic, too. At first, Ramon sat alone at lunch and couldn't find a single friend. Some of the guys started teasing him and calling him a "wetback" and other abusive words. These guys dressed differently than he was used to, listened to different music, and led entirely different lives. Ramon felt angry, alone, and helpless. It was bad enough having to move away from all his friends, but to have to put up with this, too! There were some good things about his new town, though. He liked the quietness of the country, and not having to worry about street crime or gangs anymore. He could go back and visit his friends in L.A., too.

Ramon noticed a couple of teens from his school at church, and got up the nerve to introduce himself. His new friends had other friends at school that became Ramon's new friends too, and soon even many of the teens who had teased Ramon thought he was pretty cool, even if he wasn't just like them.

Different Kinds of Different

There are lots of things that make a person "different." Even if we are all different in some way, there are groups of people that have historically been treated badly because of their disability, race, ethnicity, religion, or sexual identity. You may be part of one of these groups, or maybe — without knowing why — you just feel different.

While there is a huge amount of diversity among humans, we have much more in common with each other than we have differences. We all want to be safe, feel good, love and be loved, and be happy. We all have to eat, drink, sleep, and have shelter to survive. We all want good things for our friends and family. And we all want the freedom to be ourselves.

It is hard to understand, then, with so much in common, why there is so much violence and prejudice in the world. There is no easy answer. Many people are just fearful, and others simply don't understand the pain they cause by bullying others. Bullies are not monsters, though it may seem like it, but products of their upbringing and certain cultural attitudes that value some people over others. Many bullies have been abused in some way by their parents and this led them to abuse others.

What to Do about Bullies

Unfortunately, sometimes being different means having to learn to cope with people who don't know how to react to you — they might just keep their distance, but sometimes they act out by bullying.

Bullying can be subtle (starting a rumor about you or encouraging others to reject you) or overt (name-calling, yelling, physical assault, or even rape). Girls often bully differently than boys do, and are more apt to bully other girls in subtle ways. Boys are more likely to be bullies, and to bully using violence. Bullies can even harass you through email, websites or via instant messaging. If you have experienced any kind of bullying, or if you bully others, you are not alone. Almost 30% of U.S. teens are estimated to be involved in bullying, either as bullies, targets or both.[1]

---

1. Nansel, T.R., Overpeck, M., Pilla, R.S., Ruan, W.J., Simons-Morton, B., and Scheidt, P. (2001). Bullying behaviors among U.S. youth: Prevalence and association with psychosocial adjustment. *Journal of the American Medical Association*, 285(16), 2094–2100.

- **Tell someone**. Regardless of why bullies bully, or why society has certain longstanding prejudices against certain groups, there is something you can do about it. It is often good to talk the problem over with a supportive adult: a parent, school counselor or therapist. If the first person you tell is not receptive, then talk to another adult. If you feel that someone may actually hurt you or someone else, it is vitally important to talk to an adult that can help (you can do so anonymously, if necessary). You may feel scared or embarrassed to tell someone, or think you can handle the problem yourself, but an adult can help you game plan the situation, and adult help is essential if the bullying is more serious. This does not necessarily mean you should "tell on" the bully to get them in trouble (unless they physically hurt or steal from you) as this can let the bully know that you are upset and backfire.

- **Keep it calm**. Don't let the bully know how upset you are. Stay calm and don't retaliate. If bullies know they are getting to you, they will escalate the bullying. Respond evenly and firmly, or else say nothing and walk away. Sometimes you can even use humor to defuse the situation by making a joke or laughing at yourself.

- **Act confident**. Show the world how much you value yourself. Stand up straight, with your head up high, make eye contact, and walk confidently. A bully is less likely to target you if you project self-confidence.

- **Make friends**. Confident behavior will also improve your social success. There is strength in numbers and bullies know it — they are less likely to bully somebody that is with friends than a person who is alone. Hang out with your friends, especially at times when the bully is around. Stick up for your friends and encourage them to stand up for you also.

- **Avoid trouble situations**. If there is a place or time that you get bullied, avoid it, if possible. Avoid being alone with bullies — avoid isolated or unsupervised areas, and have your friends come along. If you get bullied on the way to school, consider a different route, leaving at a different time, or find someone to walk with you to and from school.

- **Rebuild your self-confidence**. If the bullying has affected your self-confidence or self-esteem, find activities you enjoy that can help restore your faith in yourself. Explore new interests. Make new friends that share your hobbies and interests. Get involved in extra-curricular activities (sports teams, art or hobbies, music, etc.).

- **Never resort to violence or carry a weapon**. You don't know how the bully will respond and the bully may turn a weapon against you or other people. Violence can easily escalate. Don't take the chance!

- **Being bullied is never your fault**. Bullies often pick on people who are more socially isolated or who don't project a lot of confidence. It may be easier for them to get away with picking on someone different. But being bullied doesn't have anything to do with you, it is really the bully's problem. Remember — the way people respond to you says more about them than about you.

- **How to help others being bullied**. If you can without risk to yourself, stand up for others that are being bullied. Refuse to participate in bullying others. You might try defusing the situation or trying to draw attention away from the bully. If possible, get a supportive adult to come help right away. You can encourage the bullied person to talk to an adult, or give the bullied person support by helping them up if they've been pushed down or listening to them. Include others or befriend those that are being bullied. Sit with them at lunch or offer to walk them to school. Get involved with your school's anti-bullying program, or if your school doesn't have one yet, start one. It is a lot harder for bullying to persist when other students don't participate or even discourage bullies.

- **If you bully others**. Be aware that bullying hurts others and that you don't have to participate in bullying. If you find it hard to resist bullying others, talk to an adult about how you might be able to change. Try to imagine how it feels to be bullied, and if this is difficult, ask someone supportive to help you understand the other person's side. You probably don't want others to think of you as unkind, abusive or mean and they might if you continue to bully them. Also, people don't respect bullies, they fear them. When you stop bullying, you can start gaining respect from yourself and others.

Cyber-Bullying — Texting Sticks and Stones

Sending cruel instant, text, or email messages, posting rumors or insults about a person on a website or in a blog: cyber-bullying in any form is one of the not-so-wonderful developments of our technological age. And it's so easy. After all, these bullies don't even need to be "brave" enough to attack their victims in person. Whoever first coined that old schoolyard saying: "Sticks and stones may break my bones, but words will never hurt me!" was never the victim of cyber-bullying!

If you are the victim of cyber-bullying, your first reaction may be to seek revenge, or bully that person right back, but that only fuels the fire — and gives the bully more ammunition to use against you. What can you do?

- **Block communication** with the bully.
- **Report bullying** to a trusted adult. Save all communication you receive from the bully and show it to a parent, teacher, law enforcement officer, or other adult you trust. Many schools have developed policies against this type of bullying.
- **Notify the Internet service provider** or a website moderator.

Many cyber-bullies think they are anonymous, but they can be found. Refuse to pass along their messages and don't become one yourself! Do share the National Crime Prevention Council's message with your friends:

"If you wouldn't say it in person, don't say it online. Delete cyberbullying. Don't write it. Don't forward it."

Staying Cyber-Safe

While many Internet users are friendly, it's very important to protect yourself from those who are there to hurt others. Here are some ways to stay safe:

- Never post or share your personal information online (this includes your full name, address, telephone number, school name, parents' names, credit card number, or Social Security number) or your friends' personal information.
- Never share your Internet passwords with anyone, except your parents.
- Never meet anyone face-to-face whom you only know online.
- Talk to your parents about what you do online.

(Adapted from the National Crime Prevention Council, http:/www.ncpc.org/cyberbullying)

Culture Shock

Like Ramon, you may have a different background than most of the other teens at your school. It can be more difficult to connect with others when you eat different food, watch different shows, read different books, or have different life experiences than they do. If there are cultural differences, you probably view the world differently, have different interests, or have ideas that others find strange.

It can feel lonely to be the only one who celebrates Hanukkah instead of Christmas, or who has a different color skin than most the kids at school. It can make you feel isolated or like an outsider. You may have a hard time making friends, be bullied or teased, or meet with prejudice or stereotypes based on your race, ethnicity or even your gender. These are all hard things to deal with, but good things can come out of being different, too.

Just as a stew is more flavorful and delicious with many ingredients, human experience is richer and our insights and wisdom grow through diversity. Sharing your views with others helps them think about the reasons why they believe certain things or do things a certain way; not only do you help others think and grow, but you might even learn more about yourself and feel closer to others who are different.

If You Have a Disability

Other teens can be insensitive to those with disabilities. Whether you have a learning disability, a physical difference, or a developmental disorder, others can treat you as "less-than" just on the basis of your difference. Luckily, there is now a firmly rooted disability rights movement, and people are becoming more aware of the issues that people with disabilities face.

Besides disabilities, some teens have a medical condition that changes their lives, like cancer, diabetes, or another serious illness. The stress of dealing with social problems can make coping with health issues even more difficult. Several organizations offer tips on dealing with a serious illness and networking resources so you can talk to other teens with similar issues.

- **The importance of independence.** Sometimes parents get overprotective, forgetting that teens with disabilities have the same needs that other teens have: to explore, become independent, have fun. It's important to get out and do things independently, but in a responsible way. Get involved in extracurricular activities, reach out to those with similar interests, or check into the resources of this book to find groups that help teens with disabilities meet. A lot of teens

---

"Rhianna's" Vision

Rhianna has been blind since birth. Her parents have never treated her much different from her siblings, and she's never felt there was anything wrong with how she is. During elementary school, Rhianna went to a special school for the blind. She loved her teachers and had lots of friends her own age. She and her parents agreed that she should go to a regular school for high school. She went to regular classes with all the other teens and some special classes on her own. Rhianna was surprised when the other teens seemed less than friendly. She tried a couple times to make friends with some of the other girls, but they all made it clear that they didn't want to be friends, so Rhianna sat by herself at lunch. She started to feel bad about herself, and very lonely. She talked to her parents about what she should do, and they did a web search. They found a local support group made up of local teens with disabilities. It helped to talk about her feelings with someone and to feel a sense of community with those who faced similar challenges. Her new friends came over to her house after school and the group went out together to the mall and cafe. Eventually, Rhianna made a couple of friends at her high school, some with disabilities, some without, but she feels happy at school and is preparing for a career in music.

---

with disabilities do feel excluded, but there are now more opportunities than ever to broaden your world.

- **Focus on the future**. Develop yourself, dream big, and make plans. The future is opening to people with all types of disabilities. There's no reason you can't make your dreams a reality.

- **Make the change**. High school can be a harsh environment for anyone who is slightly different, but it doesn't have to be! Some teens are changing the atmosphere of their school, and you can, too. Start a club, get involved, reach out to those who are different!

Who Am I?

We've talked about innate differences (differences people have from birth), but what about differences you choose? It's surprising how mean people can be if they don't share your taste in music or clothes. These things are often used as a social measure of "coolness." If you wear the right clothes and like the same music, according to this logic, you'll be accepted as cool; if you wear the wrong ones, sorry, you're considered a "loser." Have you ever met someone who breaks all the rules and is still accepted for who he is? While it seems like you must conform to fit in, this is not really true. People respect others who are themselves more than those who bend to popular opinion. It's important to be yourself and do what you want, but it matters how you do it. Confidence is the key.

Say you want to wear a funny hat to school . . . You're in a wacky mood. If you wear the hat, but are easily embarrassed when people make jokes about it, and keep looking at the ground and slouching, chances are that you won't get the same response that you would if you wore the hat proudly and instead teased the people who didn't like your hat.

Be who you are, and be proud!

Pressure to Dress Sexy

Girls particularly are under more and more pressure to dress very sexy. Other girls and guys may make fun of you if you don't wear tight jeans, or low-cut shirts. Somehow, our culture has decided that to be an attractive person you must be "sexy," and that means being very public about your sexuality. But a girl's worth isn't based any more on how good she looks in high heels or a short skirt than a guy's is based on how low he can wear his jeans without them falling off!

Not only is there pressure to dress sexy, there can be pressure to be casual about sex, too. It might seem cool, modern and normal to act casual about it, and decidedly uncool to be reserved. Too bad our society wants to decide for us what to wear and how to feel about sex! Our celebrities, TV shows, and music videos increasingly blare the message that "you are how you look and who you sleep with." But, just as you have the power to decide all other aspects of your self-expression (though your parents, your school and the law have some say), you have the power to take charge of your sexuality and its expression. Think about how you dress and what it means. Are you dressing to please yourself? Your parents? Your friends? Boys? Do you dress sexy because you feel you have to? How would you dress if you lived on an island by yourself? There is nothing wrong if a woman wants to show off her curves or loves wearing high heels, and there is nothing wrong if she wants to wear long sleeves, tennis shoes, and loose-fitting jeans. It's your choice, and ultimately, you're the only fashion judge you need.

Your attitude towards sex is your choice, too. There is no right attitude. If a person truly feels ready for sex, and is choosing sex in safe and healthy ways without feeling pressured, that is a legitimate choice. And for those who feel more comfortable waiting until they are married — or in a monogamous, loving relationship — that is another choice to respect. The important thing is that you honor your values and desires, and don't make important decisions based on a desire to "be cool." Whoever you are, *that's* truly cool!

Sundays, Saturdays, or Not at All?

Religion can be a very emotional issue, since religion defines how we think of the universe and how we see good and evil, right and wrong. If your religion is the minority where you live, others may not understand your religion (or lack thereof) and associate it with stereotypes or myths. After 9/11, many Muslims became targets of violence and prejudice, and some people continue to make judgments against all Muslims based on fear and ignorance, instead of seeing that most Muslims are not violent and worship similarly to Jews and Christians. Some people wear religious symbols or garments that look "weird" to outsiders: some female Muslims wear a chador, some male Sikhs wear a kirpan, Buddhists may shave their heads, or Jewish boys might wear a yarmulke. It can also be difficult for atheists and religious people to understand each other.

It's clear that a lot of conflict is caused when people of different religions don't practice tolerance of others. You can help spread tolerance and understanding instead of judgment and hatred by learning about other religions. You might find that other religions are not so very different from your own. Everyone has a right to be respected for their choices and beliefs. Whether someone doesn't believe in God or believes in different gods, you can still be friendly to each other and you might even learn something! As humans we are all trying to make sense of our existence, and — since there is so much we don't know — we've come to several different conclusions.

Your Beliefs

Your beliefs may be different from your parents'. Maybe you are liberal on political issues and they are conservative. Or maybe you believe that art is the only thing that matters, while they want you to be a doctor or an engineer. This can be very difficult for both you and your parents. You may feel that your parents are rigid or uptight, and be angry that they don't understand you. They might worry that your beliefs will endanger you, and often feel they are being good parents by guiding your choices causing them to seem too strict.

Soon you will be a fully autonomous adult and be responsible for all your decisions. This can be scary, but also liberating. What this means is that, ultimately, you are the only one who can decide who you want to be. You have the right to believe, feel and experience the world exactly as you do, and you get to choose your values. So if you disagree with your parents, while you must abide by your parent's rules while you live with them, soon you'll be on your own and then you will be the one who makes your decisions. You can also:

- **Educate others**. Your parent's concern might have to do with a lack of information on the subject. If, for instance, you have decided to become a professional dancer and your parent worries that you might seriously hurt your health, do some research that will put her mind at ease, or if you want to volunteer for a political candidate, show your parents what this candidate has in common with their values. Most of the time, showing your parents that you are responsible and take your choices seriously will be enough to garner their support, but sometimes they will still refuse consent. If this happens, tell them how important your autonomy is to you and that you want to learn responsibility now before you become an adult. Sometimes however, if your parents are very threatened by a new idea — for instance, if you are atheist and you know your parents will be extremely upset or even violent in their reactions — it may be best to keep the idea to yourself for the time being. It is important to always be true to yourself, but sometimes it is best not to share that truth with others if you think they will harm you. While is not your responsibility to educate others, it might help them understand where you're coming from, and increase their tolerance of people like you.

- **Be yourself**. Regardless of how your parents or friends react, you can keep believing what you want and being who you are. It isn't always easy being yourself, but it's better than the alternative: living a lie or being someone you're not so that other people will be happy with you. It isn't necessary to tell everyone everything about you — you can use your judgment about who to tell, but you can still be proud of who you are, even if not everyone will understand.

- **Be confident**. It can be hard being the only one of something at your school. If your classmates have never met a Hindu or if you're the only Green Party supporter at your school, it can be difficult to feel part of things. By being proud of who you are you let other people know that being Muslim, vegetarian, or gay isn't scary. Your confidence might even inspire others to feel free to be different also.

- **Connect with all kinds of people**. You can help the social climate for everyone by being friends with as many kinds of people as possible. Don't be afraid of befriending someone just because they dress preppy while you dress punk, or because they go to temple while you sleep in on Saturday mornings. If you hear someone repeating a stereotype or criticizing someone just based on a category, you can tell them to knock it off and to grow some compassion!

"I have a friend that is different"

If you have a friend who is "different" you may get teased or be pressured to stop hanging out with him. Or maybe your friend just told you something new about herself or has started to dress differently, hang out with new people, or act differently than she did before. Think about your feelings: How do you feel? Uncomfortable? Disgusted? Weirded-out? Don't be afraid of your feelings — we all have feelings that we aren't proud of. If your friend has changed in some way that you don't like, try to see it from his point of view. Why did she change? Will she be happier now? Is some prejudice of your own getting in the way of accepting your friend?

Everyone has a right to change, to embrace life as they see fit, and to decide who they are. Our job as friends is to treat them with kindness no matter what! If your friend changes you may find that you don't have a lot in common anymore and that you don't enjoy that person's company any longer — that's okay and happens to some friendships anyway, but guard against hasty, angry behavior you'll regret like name-calling, rumor-spreading, or isolating. Your friend has confided in you, and you owe her the decency to at least treat her with respect!

Feelings are just feelings. They should be acknowledged, but you can decide which ones to act upon. Inside all of our heads, our society's prejudices filter down and inform our thoughts. Unless we've made an effort to weed them out, we all have some racist, sexist or homophobic ideas. We all know about ethnic stereotypes and if we have a bad experience with a person from a particular group, a stereotypical thought about that group might come up. Being a compassionate person doesn't mean that we never have these thoughts, it means that we are aware of our prejudices and make every effort not to act on them. It is impossible to stop all such thoughts and feelings — until we live in a prejudice-less society — but it is always possible to act with compassion. Acting with compassion starts when we put ourselves into other people's shoes and see them as fully human. Think about what their lives have been like, how they are the same as you, and how they might be different.

Accepting differences in our friends and communities allows everyone to fully be who they are and for us to celebrate the dignity and worthiness of all different kinds of people.

We're all different! Wouldn't it be great if we could all learn to accept our differences? There are a lot of difficulties in growing up even without special challenges. This is the time of life where you have to figure out who you're going to be, separate from your parents, and set your course for life! But this transition becomes much harder when you are dealing with issues like gender or sexual identity, having a disability, being bullied, or having strict parents who don't understand the person you're becoming. Take heart because no matter how tough things are, you will learn from your experiences and someday you will be living a life that's authentically yours!

The Difference Is...

- **Learn to protect yourself** and develop the skills you need to stay safe and deal with people who have trouble accepting your differences, such as bullies.

- **Educate others** if you can, since people's negative reactions often come from fear of something they don't understand.

- **Be confident**. If you are comfortable being who you are and show that confidence in yourself through your behavior and actions, other people will be more likely to be comfortable with it, too!

- **Connect/make friends/reach out**. Don't expect others to approach or reach out to you. Make the effort to connect with them so that they can get to know how great you are!

Chapter 5

"Are You Having Fun Yet?"
(Feeling Good)

There are many things you can do for yourself, without using drugs, to keep yourself feeling good. Here's our list of the basic essentials. You can add to this list as you discover nice things you can do for yourself to keep up your spirits:

- **Work up a sweat.** Exercise every day, fifteen minutes or more. You need to work hard enough at it to get a little sweaty. Make it FUN. Exercise actually produces chemicals in your body that make you feel good. You'll notice how much better you feel afterward. (You can jog, climb a mountain, ride your bike or skateboard, dance, play tug-of-war with your dog, jump rope, play sports with your friends.)

- **Think positive thoughts.** Focus your mind on the good things in your life, the things you like about yourself, the things you enjoy doing. Try to capture the good feelings they give you so you can remember them when you need to.

- **Find a listener.** Find a friend who'll listen to you without judging you. This person needs to accept you just the way you are and be willing to listen without giving advice, unless you ask for it.

- **Relax!** Relaxation relieves stress. You can keep yourself calm, alert, aware and feeling competent and capable. When you are upset, really look at something and describe it to yourself in detail. How many different colors can you find in it? What about textures? Does it have a taste, an odor, a sound? You'll feel better because you'll have left the past and not gone into the future. You're exploring the present.

More Ways to Relax:

- Take a deep breath, let it out slowly — repeat 10 times or more.

- Lie down and close your eyes: now tighten every muscle in your body — curl your toes, clench your teeth, make fists — hold that for a few seconds. Now let all your muscles relax, imagine each muscle getting loose and warm — work from your toes to the top of your head until your whole body feels relaxed.

- **Go for natural highs.** You can keep yourself feeling good without man-made chemicals. The really great high times in your life can be from being relaxed, enjoying nature, winning a race, achieving a goal, accomplishing something, being in a place where you can see beauty. There are lots of natural highs out there for you — and they need no drugs!

- **Be grateful!** Take a few minutes to relax your body. Think of the things in your life you're grateful for. Write down this list and keep adding to it. If you feel depressed, make a new list. Be sure to include things you like about your parents, friends, your body, fun times, special people in your life, important events like birthdays and holidays.

- **Make a lovable list.** When you focus on the good things about yourself, your life changes tremendously. Make a list of things you like about yourself (skills, talents, strengths). Make sure each item is positive. Don't say things like, "Sometimes I feel good about myself." Say, "I like myself."

Make it a very long list. Pages. If you have trouble getting started, ask a friend, a parent, a brother or sister to help you. Say, "What are the things you like about me?" Write everything down.

- I am lovable and valuable.
- I like myself.
- I am a good person.
- I am intelligent and capable.
- I am my own best friend.
- People like me.
- I am in charge of my life.
- I have many strengths and talents.
- I'm happy with the way I handle myself around others.

Now write down the things you like about your body. (I have a friend who loves her ear lobes!) Write down your best school subjects, your favorite sports, your favorite things to do, when you did something you were particularly proud of (and remember how it felt!). Don't stop; keep adding to your list. Say it to yourself while you are getting dressed, walking to school, or waiting for a friend. Keep your list in a place where you can look at it a lot, at home on the wall above your desk, or in the drawer near your bed. If you wake up in the morning feeling bad, read your list until you feel GOOD.

- **Store your compliments.** Take a paper bag, or get a shoebox and cut a slit in the top. Mark it "COMPLIMENTS." Each time someone gives you a compliment, write it down on a slip of paper and store it in your Compliment Bag or Box. When you are feeling bad, get out the box. Read compliments until you feel GOOD.

- **Dream a dream.** Many of us are stingy with ourselves. In focusing on our faults we neglect building our futures. When you dream about the kind of life you would like *take yourself seriously*. Make your dream amazing. Make it big. Make it worthy of you. Why not? Be generous with yourself. Give yourself all the things you would like to have. Dreams are free. Life's pretty boring without them. If you don't have a dream of your own you'll find yourself following someone else's. You'll be working for them, using their ideas, helping with their inventions. Why not be the leader, the inventor, the builder, the idea person?

- **Make a movie of your life.** Turn your phone off, close the door and get comfortable. Relax your body. Give yourself some time to let your imagination run wild. You're in Hollywood. You're the script writer, the director, the star and the casting director. Select a script, write it, choose your supporting stars and actors, set the scene and direct it! Go ahead. Make it exciting and wonderful. If you don't like the way it is going, start over. Create a new movie.

- **Help others.** This might sound pretty strange..., "How can I help other people when I can hardly handle my own life?!" you might wonder. But, whether you volunteer on a regular basis — maybe at a local animal shelter, hospital, or homeless shelter — or simply offer a hand to a friend or neighbor in need, helping others helps you feel better about yourself. Not comfortable working with people? There are a lot of things you can do to help our planet or your local environment, too: pick up trash, participate in a local beach or creek clean-up day, plant bushes or trees at a local Arbor Day celebration, or get involved in a city's beautification efforts. (For more ideas, see www.earthday.net.)

- **"Mirror, mirror…"** See yourself standing in front of a full-length mirror. Look at yourself the way you are right now. Now let those lines blur and change until you look the way you'd like. See yourself moving, talking gesturing, looking alive and happy. Add ten years. How do you look? See yourself move with greater confidence, gesture, see the expression on your face. How do you talk? Add another ten years. Increase your power, talent, and skills each time. When you reach middle age, see yourself healthy and active. As you grow older, imagine keeping busy and productive and continuing to grow in knowledge, skills and abilities. Imagine starting a new career when everyone else is retiring. See yourself actively involved in sports. Imagine yourself surrounded by friends and family. See them all adoring you. Now come back to the present time. Isn't your life great? Aren't *you* great?

When You Just Can't Seem to Feel Better

We've told you about lots of ways you can make yourself feel better. After all, everyone can feel down or depressed at times. But when that depressed feeling just won't go away, or becomes more intense than you can handle, you may actually suffer from depression. The good news is that it is treatable and you have more control over it than you might think; but it is also more *common* than you might guess — as many as 20% of students will be affected before graduating from high school (according to The American Psychological Association's website: http://www.psychologymatters.org/gillham.html).

Not all people have the same symptoms of depression, nor do they have the symptoms as often or for the same lengths of time. Symptoms can vary from person to person; here are some of the common symptoms of teen depression:

- Loss of interest in activities or hobbies that once were fun
- Irritability, restlessness

- Social withdrawal — Spending a majority of time alone and avoiding the company of others
- Sleep problems — Insomnia, or excessive sleeping
- Difficulty in school — Having a hard time concentrating, remembering details or making decisions
- Vague physical complaints — These might include headaches, stomach aches, or feeling constantly tired
- Persistent sad, anxious or "empty" feelings — Not caring
- Feelings of hopelessness and/or pessimism
- Feelings of guilt, worthlessness and/or helplessness
- Overeating, or appetite loss
- Thoughts of suicide, suicide attempts

(Adapted from *You Can Beat Depression*, Dr. John Preston, Impact Publishers, Inc., 2004, and the National Institute of Mental Health's website: www.nimh.nih.gov)

Get Help, Now!

If you are thinking about harming yourself, or know someone who is, tell someone who can help immediately.

- Call your doctor.
- Call 911 or go to a hospital emergency room to get immediate help or ask a friend or family member to help you do these things.
- Call the toll-free, 24-hour hotline of the National Suicide Prevention Lifeline at 1-800-273-TALK (1-800-273-8255); TTY: 1-800-799-4TTY (4889) to talk to a trained counselor.
- Make sure you or the suicidal person is not left alone.

If you think a friend may be depressed, it can affect you too. The first and most important thing you can do to help a friend or relative who has depression is to help him get professional help from a doctor or therapist. Then:

- Offer your support, understanding, patience and encouragement.
- Involve your friend or relative in conversation, and listen carefully.
- Never put down the feelings your friend or relative talks about, but point out realities and offer hope.
- Never ignore comments about suicide, and report them to your friend's relatives or an adult who can help.
- Invite your friend or relative out for walks, outings and other activities. Keep trying if she declines, but don't push her to take on too much too soon.
- Remind your friend or relative that with time and treatment, the depression will lift.

Don't expect to be able to "cure" your friend yourself, though. People with depression need help from trained professionals.

I Feel Good!

Feeling good has a lot to do with your attitude, activities and thoughts about yourself. Find out what works for you:

- Physically — Exercise, but learn to relax, too.
- Mentally — Focus on the positive things in your life so that you can turn your thoughts to them when you need an attitude adjustment.
- Emotionally — Find a listener that you can really talk to without feeling self-conscious. Become aware of what makes you feel good so that you can remember that feeling when you need to feel better.
- Get help — If you have depressed feelings that last, go to a counselor or other trusted adult that can help you get the treatment you need.

Chapter 6

Listen Up!
(Assertiveness)

You just found out that your best friend is smoking pot and taking pills — a lot. What are you going to do?

You could get mad and blow up at him:

"You jerk! You are *so* dumb! How can you be so stupid? Next thing I know you'll be failing three classes and getting dropped from the team. You're throwing your life away and burning out your brain. But you're not going to ruin *my* reputation — there's no way I'm hanging around to watch you blow it."

Or, you could find some time alone with him and say:

"I've heard you've been smoking pot and taking pills with Josh and it really scares me. I mean, I know pot takes away your ambition and pills can destroy your brain. I feel like I'm losing my best friend and it really makes me sad."

The first response puts your friend down without helping him.

The second response talks about your own feelings without making judgments or calling your friend names. You'll have more luck getting your friend to listen and talk to you when you're being honest and direct, without putting him down. (Notice the switch from "you..." statements to "I..." statements.) You can't force anyone to do what you want. You need to be prepared to let your friend go, or try to live with his problem. You can let him know you're upset. You can decide not to *help* him hurt himself. You can say that you won't help by covering up or lying. Or you can just keep your ideas to yourself and try to avoid the situation. The choices are yours.

We have seen a lot of teens handle such tough choices successfully by being *assertive*. Assertiveness is taking charge of your life: speaking clearly and honestly, asking for what you want and saying no to what you don't want. It is learning to feel valuable, capable and powerful. In other words, it is *really caring* about yourself. But, the assertive person helps others feel good about themselves too, by treating them in loving, caring, kind, thoughtful ways.

Assertiveness helps you achieve your goals — but it won't tell you what your goals should be.

Who Is Assertive?

To be assertive means...

- to speak honestly.
- to expect to be treated with respect and to treat others that way.
- to like yourself.
- to stand up for and take good care of yourself.
- to be a friend to others.
- to keep your cool and sense of humor in order to handle situations smoothly.

Assertive Body Language
- calm, pleasant facial expression
- direct eye contact
- relaxed body, good posture
- firm voice
- confident gestures

"The Sweater"

Lindsay is walking down the hall at school. Her friend Michelle rushes up bubbling happily about her date with a new guy she likes, Ian. She asks Lindsay, "Can I wear your new pink sweater Saturday? It'd look great with my black skirt. I'll take good care of it."

Lindsay doesn't want to lend out her new sweater. What does she tell Michelle?

- Stammering and blushing, her stomach tightening into knots: "Oh sure, Michelle. You can wear it." Lindsay gets a stomachache, goes home and feels sick all night.

—OR—

- Angrily, her face turning red: "I can't even believe you'd ask me that! You know that's my favorite sweater and it's brand new, too! What makes you think I'd want to lend it to you?!"

—OR—

- Honestly and directly: "Michelle, you're my best friend and I don't want to hurt your feelings, but that sweater is my favorite and I'm not going to lend it out. I hope you understand and won't be mad at me. You know, your new outfit looks terrific on you — you could wear that, couldn't you?"

When Lindsay reluctantly agrees to let Michelle borrow her sweater she's being *passive*: letting people walk all over her because she's afraid to speak up for what she wants.

Lindsay's angry overreaction is *aggressive*: hurting people or putting them down because she doesn't know how (or is afraid) to honestly say what she wants.

The last response is *assertive*: Lindsay is straightforward and calm in telling Michelle how she feels.

Dealing with people assertively is usually your best choice; contrasting it with other styles might help show why.

Aggressive People Are Like Steamrollers — Flattening Down People in Their Way

Aggressive people get what they want by:

- putting people down; calling them names, saying mean things.
- hurting people physically or emotionally.
- pushing people around physically, mentally or emotionally.
- telling people what to do, forcibly taking charge, making people do things against their will.
- making all the rules without listening to others' ideas.
- interrupting people.

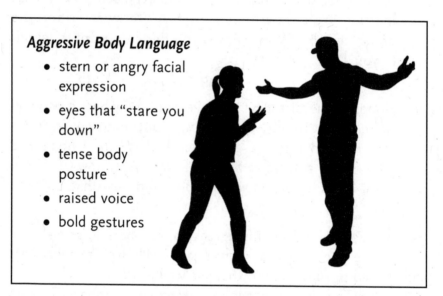

Aggressive Body Language
- stern or angry facial expression
- eyes that "stare you down"
- tense body posture
- raised voice
- bold gestures

The "steamroller" flattens anyone who gets in the way; others feel weak, small, or helpless because she is always taking charge. Aggressiveness can cause you to lose your self-confidence and feel bad about yourself. Most people don't like being around someone who's being aggressive. They'd rather totally avoid such a person.

Lots of people get mad when they're pushed around. The aggressive person is surprised at people's anger. She doesn't pay attention to other people's feelings, so doesn't realize she's hurting them. You can let aggressive people know you're hurt or angry by saying: "What you just said really hurt my feelings," or "I really don't like it when you tell me what to do," or "I'd rather make up my own mind, thanks," or "You can call me a 'dork' or any other name you want to, but I'm not gonna let you push me into doing drugs."

Passive People Act Like Doormats

Passive behavior is doing nothing, playing it safe, keeping your mouth closed. It is being a doormat: letting others walk on you. Other people make decisions for you, tell you what to do and run your life.

The passive person:

- doesn't stand up for himself.
- waits for others to make decisions.
- keeps quiet even when he knows the correct answer or the best action to take.
- would rather do anything than ask for a favor, help, or what he wants.
- withdraws, stands back, makes no waves.

Passive Body Language
- face looks sad, shy or frightened
- avoids eye contact
- shoulders droop
- voice is soft and wobbly

Passive people often get pushed around, "stepped on" or forgotten. Other people often take advantage of them because they rarely stand up for themselves. The passive person usually has a poor self-image, and little self-confidence.

Passive-Aggressive People Are "The Gotcha Group"

Passive-aggressive people think they're "nice," but they're usually really angry because they hardly ever get what they want. They:

- aren't honest about their feelings with themselves or others.
- store up anger and wait, planning revenge.
- "get even" in subtle ways (they're "late" or they "forget").
- leave you wondering what happened.

Passive-Aggressive Body Language
- face may be smiling, but it seems fake
- eye contact varies with their mood (may be "wide-eyed/innocent" as if to say "who me?")
- gestures often don't match their words

Here's a passive-aggressive example.

Marianne is getting ready for a ski trip that Shannon would love to go on, but can't afford:

Marianne: "Shannon, since you're not going skiing with us would you mind feeding my goldfish while I'm gone?"

Shannon: "Well, okay — I guess I could."

Marianne: "Great! Thanks a lot!"

Marianne returns from her trip one week later to find her fish dead; Shannon "accidentally" overfed them.

Usually people act aggressively, passively or passive-aggressively because they are afraid or don't know how to openly express how they feel. Of course, few of us fit neatly into any category — but if you can start seeing yourself "steamrolling," or playing "doormat" or "gotcha," you're learning to be honest with yourself — a big step on your way toward assertiveness.

You Can Learn Assertiveness...

...it's not something you have to be born with. There are several steps:

Learning

- to like yourself
- to know and stand up for your rights
- to be responsible
- to ask for what you want
- to say no without feeling guilty
- to handle stress and anxiety (learning to relax)
- to use your personal power
- to deal with criticism in positive ways (Some people are afraid to be assertive because they're afraid of being criticized. If you learn to listen only to *useful* criticism, you don't need to feel attacked or put down. You can use criticism to grow!)
- to give and receive compliments easily (Don't deny compliments, or feel you have to return them — you can accept them with a smile and a "thank you.")
- to show anger honestly, not aggressively, without hurting others (and to let others express anger toward you)
- to avoid being manipulated
- to have (and keep) friendships and loving relationships

Assertive Listening

Communicating assertively means learning to listen well, too. If you don't give the other person the opportunity to speak up, then you are not having a conversation — you're giving a speech! Assertive listening is:

- showing respect for the other person by giving her your full attention without interrupting
- making good eye contact, and an effort to understand what she is saying
- responding only after you've really considered the message.

After all, why should anyone listen to what you have to say if you won't do the same?

Some Tips for Learning Assertiveness

Role-playing can help you feel more comfortable being assertive — it's a good way to practice your assertiveness skills.

- Write a script that spells out what you want to say and what the other person might say in response.
- Practice with a mirror, a friend or a video camera until you look and sound just the way you want.
- Have a friend help by reading your script to you, taking your part and letting you see how you look and sound.
- Have your friend make suggestions.
- Take turns playing yourself and the person you'll be talking to.

Speaking Up and Staying Safe

An important part of learning to be assertive is knowing when to be assertive . . . and when to walk away. We used to say, "Stand up for yourself!" "Don't be afraid to speak out!" "Don't let people push you around!" And it used to be safe to do that. Now you need to look at the situation first: who are you dealing with? Is this a dangerous person or situation? Trust your feelings. If you're really scared for your safety, then walk (or run!) away. Don't put yourself in unnecessary danger in order to act assertively. If someone is pointing a gun at you and demanding your money — give it to him! The assertive choice here is not to speak up to this dangerous person, but to try to stay calm . . . and report him to the police as soon as possible! Often, choosing to get out of a bad situation is the assertive choice — because your safety comes first.

Kindly Stand Up

Assertiveness means treating other people with kindness and respect, standing up for your rights, and respecting the rights of others. You can achieve your goals without taking anything away from anyone.

Assertiveness is not judging others. It is being yourself, and letting others be themselves. The only person you can take responsibility for is YOU. You're the only one who can make your life good, productive and useful.

Standing up for your rights isn't easy the first time. It gets more and more exciting every time you try it, and you like yourself better all the time. You can and do have power over your life. You have hundreds of choices always.

That's What I Want!

Learning assertiveness doesn't happen overnight but is a skill that builds up slowly. Start out with easy things and little-by-little add harder things. Each time you do something assertive you'll feel good. When you start asking for what you want you'll be amazed: people LIKE to give you what you want! As you get more assertive, you respect yourself and others respect you. It's easier to be honest and you like yourself more.

Practice:

- asking for what you want
- saying no
- speaking clearly and honestly

Chapter 7

When You Get *So* Mad
(Dealing with Anger)

What do you do when you're mad? Punch a pillow? Yell at your younger brother or sister? Slam your door and crank up your iPod? Do you tell people when you're angry? Or do you let your body language (clenched fists, stomping around) speak for you? Or maybe you don't show your anger at all. Some people are raised to believe that it's not OK to show your anger — that you should hold it inside because it's not "nice" to get angry with people. Unfortunately, that held-in anger usually just shows up in other ways — like an upset stomach, a headache, or trouble sleeping. That doesn't mean that you have to show your anger to make it go away — you aren't a balloon that will pop if you don't let it out. In fact, behaving in an angry way can actually make you more angry! So punching that pillow isn't the best solution — especially if you're imagining someone's face in it — you might just want to hit it more, or harder!

What can you do about your anger? The best solution is to **take charge** of your anger before it builds. If it's too late for that, you'll need to **find a solution** to your problem — in this case, whatever it is that has you feeling so *mad*.

55

From Mad to Mean — by Melissa

One of my best friends in junior high and high school was extremely loyal — she put up with my moods, was there when I needed her, and stuck by me no matter what. Still, one day I was so angry with her that I wouldn't talk to her. I made sure that I was extra-nice to everybody else that I saw that day, so she would be sure to know that it was she alone with whom I was furious. Finally, during P.E. at the end of the day, she burst into tears and yelled at me, "I hate it when you're like this! I'd rather have you just yell at me and get it over with than not talk to me! You're not even giving me a chance to apologize!" I still can't remember why I was so mad at my friend that day. But I don't think I'll ever forget the look on her face — and how awful I felt for really hurting a true friend. How much better it would have been for both of us if I'd been straight with her and told her how I felt right away!

Taking Charge

Say somebody accidentally steps on a homework paper of yours that you worked on for hours. Your teacher is a "neat freak" and won't be happy about how it looks now. Are you angry? How angry? When you feel your anger starting to build, ask yourself, "How much does this really matter? Is it worth my getting upset? Will I even care about it two weeks from now? Two days from now? Two *hours* from now?"

It's a lot easier to stop your anger from building than it is to calm down after you've gotten really mad, and there are a couple of ways you can help yourself do that:

- **Stop and "rate" your anger.** Sure, some things are worth getting upset about. If someone steals your bike, you're probably going to be pretty mad (or maybe sad, too). It's a bad thing, right? So, on an "upset" scale from one to ten, it's about a six or a seven . . . After all, there are worse things that could happen. Your home could be robbed, and everything you own stolen. That's worse. How would you rate it? An eight? What if a drunk driver killed someone you care about? That's really terrible — probably a ten. So, let's step back for a second . . . is it really that big of a deal that he stepped on your paper? How would you rate it now?

- **Save yourself a lot of anger by stepping outside yourself and looking at things from the other person's point of view.** We've all had those mornings . . . You know: you wake up late; can't find the shirt you wanted to wear; somebody ate the last of the good cereal; you forgot your math paper was due today, and it's not done; your mom yelled at you . . . So now you're *really* late, and you run out the door and right into a neighbor on the sidewalk . . . How angry should your neighbor be? Does he know how your morning is going, or does he just think you're some careless kid mowing down everybody who gets in your way? He can choose to get angry, or not to let it upset him. What would you do if you were in his place?

- **Try to give the other person a break.** Did that lady turn her car right in front of you because she didn't care if she hit you and your bike, or was it because she just found out that a friend is in the hospital and she's just not seeing clearly right now? Did your dad slam the door because he's *trying* to make your headache worse, or did he just step in the "present" your neighbor's dog left on the porch?

- **Be creative!** Maybe that guy cut in front of you in line because aliens abducted him last night and turned his brains to spaghetti . . .

- **Find the humor in the situation.** Once, while driving, Melissa began to get frustrated with the driver of the car in front of her (who seemed to be paying more attention to his frisky dog than to the road): "So, I joked with my family, 'He should let his dog drive — the chihuahua would probably do a better job!' We laughed at the image of the tiny dog trying to drive the car, and I found my frustration going away." A good laugh does wonders for a bad mood!

You'll always feel better about yourself if you can make the best of a bad situation — instead of letting *it* get the best of *you*.

Finding a Solution

There are times, of course, when you will be angry and need to deal with that anger appropriately. It's not always easy. Here are some helpful guidelines you can use to try to stay in charge of your anger:

- **Pay attention to what things tend to bother you.** See if you can avoid your angry feelings by being aware of your emotions and working toward a solution. For example, if you always get irritated at the pushing and shoving in the line at the cafeteria, then choose to eat there less often (get up earlier and make your lunch), or talk to school officials to see if the staff can help control the situation. Better yet, work on your own attitude: "I know, I'm going to get bumped around in line, so I'm going to take deep breaths and try to stay relaxed and calm."

- **Learn how your body reacts to anger.** You can identify what happens with your body as you begin to get angry, and learn how to control your reactions. Think about a time that you were very angry. (Try not to do this very often, remembering a time when you were very upset can renew that old anger and make you angry all over again. You're just doing this now for this exercise.) Picture the scene in your mind, and concentrate on what is happening to your body. Is your heart rate speeding up? Do you feel your face getting hot? Are your teeth clenched?

Are your muscles tightening? These are signals that are helpful for you to recognize, so that you can use your "taking charge" skills to deal with the situation.

- **Learn to relax when you are feeling angry.** Now, tighten every muscle in your body that you can — hard! Hold it for a count of ten, and then let every muscle relax. Roll your head on your shoulders and take several deep, slow breaths in and out. (See chapter 5, "Feeling Good," for more tips on relaxation.) Think about a time when you were happy, and let go of your angry feelings.

- **Express your anger assertively.** Of course, there are times when it is appropriate to express your anger, as long as you do it assertively (not aggressively). If you think the situation will be improved by your speaking up, go ahead and do it. Remember the assertiveness skills we discussed in chapter 6, "Listen Up," and speak honestly using "I" statements and staying as relaxed as possible (It may help to practice in front of a mirror or with a friend first, paying attention to your words, body language, and tone of voice.): "Kirsten, I'm really mad that you went out with Alex. He was my boyfriend, and I feel like I can't trust you anymore. It's hard for me to be around you now, so I'll be changing study groups. I hope you understand."

- **Think about what is causing your anger.** It may help you to realize that anger comes from not getting our needs met. When we make sure our own needs are met then we do not need to be angry or depressed. Sometimes just understanding *why* you are feeling the way you are (Are you hungry? Tired? Lonely? Frustrated?) helps you take charge of *how* you are feeling.

Other People's Anger

Dealing with your own anger is difficult enough, but coping with the anger of others can be even harder. The same skills can work for both, though: Be honest and direct. Try to stay calm and relaxed and avoid aggression (yours or the other person's!). You can't control how other people feel, but you can keep from making the situation worse by overreacting. You can always choose to walk away; often that's the best way to stop adding "fuel to the fire."

Anger can go hand-in-hand with violence, especially when emotions get out of control. When the first edition of *Teen Esteem* came out, there hadn't been the teen violence we've now seen in school shootings in Jonesboro, Arkansas; Columbine, Colorado; Roanoke, Virginia . . . Sure, violence was easy to find — it was there on TV every night just as it is now, but somehow it didn't seem so close. It was on the streets, in other countries or neighborhoods . . . out *there* somewhere for many of us.

Now, violence is everywhere . . . in video and convenience stores, fast food places, the music on the radio . . . *schools*; not only inner-city schools, but small town and rural schools. It's unpredictable, sudden, and scary. So, most of us don't think about it — or we try not to, because it makes us uncomfortable. But violence can catch up to you when you're not paying attention.

So we talk about it, and try to teach ways to avoid it — but the only thing we really know is that *we don't know* when or where it will happen, and that means we have to prepare for it . . . because in any situation if you are able to relax enough to think clearly, you may well be able to find a way to safety.

The best way to escape violence is to avoid it. Safety programs across the United States tell us that we should:

- Avoid situations (with places or people) that you know are dangerous.

- Stay away from guns, knives, and other weapons. If a friend has one, leave immediately or insist he put it away. (See also the last item on this list.)

- Always walk quickly, with confidence.

- Avoid gangs.
- Avoid giving out your phone number or address to strangers.
- Carry yourself with pride. Don't look like a victim.
- Avoid being alone in isolated areas.
- Go to the nearest open business or familiar home, if you think you're being followed.
- Yell "Fire!" if you are attacked; yelling "Help!" can scare people away.
- Check inside and under your car before getting in it after it has been parked.
- Keep doors locked and windows up when driving at night.
- Drive to the nearest police station if you are followed when driving; don't go home.
- Pair up with someone you trust if you are going out after dark. Tell an adult where you are going.
- If you know someone is considering violence (against themselves or others), tell someone who can help.

Violence can't always be avoided, but if you stay alert and trust your instincts (those little hairs on the back of your neck....), you'll be doing your part in keeping yourself safe. Part of feeling good about yourself is having the confidence in yourself to know that you can make smart choices and handle or avoid dangerous situations.

The "Method to Your Mad-ness"

None of us *always* feels in control over our emotions, and anger is certainly a powerful feeling to handle. Here are some key points to remember to help you deal with it effectively:

- **Take charge** of your anger by stopping it from building *before* you get too worked up. Use some of the tips we discussed in this chapter: rating your anger, looking at things from another's point of view, giving others a break, being creative, finding the humor in the situation.

- **Find a solution** to problem situations by paying attention to what usually bothers you, recognizing how your body reacts to it, and then learning to relax through it or assertively express yourself.

- **Anger can lead to violence**. The best way to escape violence is to avoid situations where it is likely to occur. If that's not possible, trust your instincts, carry yourself with confidence, and try to relax enough to think clearly.

Some of the information in this chapter was adapted from *Your Perfect Right: Assertiveness and Equality in Your Life and Relationships*, © 2008 by Robert E. Alberti and Michael L. Emmons. Impact Publishers, Inc., Atascadero, California.

Chapter 8

Asking for It
(Making Requests)

Can you remember going to someone's house when you were a kid and standing looking at a candy jar? You were told by your mother not to ask for *anything*. When you were hungry you might have sucked on your thumb, but couldn't ask for food.

Once your parents succeeded in making you into a creature that they could take out to visit with their friends, you were properly "socialized." Now, however, you may have to unlearn some of those early lessons to become assertive. For example, it's okay to ask for what you want — and you don't need to feel guilty about it.

Good News

You can ask for ANYTHING you want from ANYONE — and anyone over the age of two can say "no" to you! Some people aren't able to say no directly, but they generally won't do anything that goes against their personal safety, morals or beliefs. They find other ways to avoid it. How many people you know will jump off a high building just because you tell them to? You can trust that sane, drug-free people *will* take care of themselves.

If you ask in a direct way, you give people the chance to answer honestly. For instance, you'd like to invite a good-looking guy or girl you don't know very well to a party. You could say, "Rosa, I want to invite you to go with me to Kayla's party on Saturday, but I don't know how you feel about big crowded parties, and I'm not sure if there'll be drinking and drugs. Do you

63

want to go? If not, I totally understand. Maybe we could go to the movies instead."

You let Rosa be in control of her choice by showing you care about her values. She'll appreciate your concern for her feelings.

Asking for What You Want

What happens when you ask someone for something? Do you think that if you ask, people will feel that they have to give you what you want? Are you afraid of being rejected? What thoughts hold you back from asking? Writing them down could help you recognize them.

Here are some thoughts that keep people from asking for what they want:

"They won't like me anymore."
"He won't love me if I ask for what I want."
"If I ask, she'll think I'm greedy."
"It's rude to ask."
"Polite people don't ask."
"They should know what I want."
"Asking is pushy."
"People who ask for things are spoiled."

Read each one carefully. Have any of them ever stopped you from asking for something you wanted? Was it realistic or just something you used to scare yourself? Would your father actually faint if you asked him for a hug? Would he think you're a sissy? Would your friend hate you if you asked for help doing math? Would she think you're dumb?

Learning to recognize those thoughts that are scaring you away from what you want will help you stop them from holding you back.

Your Friends Aren't Mind-Readers!

"I don't need to ask. If I wait long enough, they'll offer it to me." "If they love me, they'll know what I want." "Maybe someone will notice I'm dying of thirst." "I hope they give me some too." "Why are they so lucky and I never get anything I want?"

You can't be sure people will know what you want *unless* you ask!

Practice Asking

Asking for things is easier when you have practice doing it. Here are some sentences to practice:

- Please stop tapping my seat.
- Please be quiet so I can study.
- Would you please put out your cigarette? It's against the law to smoke in an elevator.
- When you pick me up late, I get really upset. Would you please come on time?
- Your music is bothering me. Please turn it down.
- I like you a lot, but when you pressure me to sleep with you, I wonder if you really care about me. Would you stop talking about it?
- I'm feeling lonely. Would you come over to my house after school?
- Would you go to the movies with me on Saturday?
- Would you like to study for the test with me tomorrow?
- Do you want to go to my house and shoot some baskets?
- Dad, can we go fishing together this weekend?
- Mom, will you show me how to make my favorite pie?
- How about all of us going camping next summer?
- Can we have a party for my birthday?
- I would really like to go to school at . . . Would you mind if I were so far away?

Getting What You Want

When you ask for things you accomplish your goals. You don't have to pretend to be big and strong and capable of meeting *all* your own needs. Human beings need each other. It's O.K. for you to be human. You don't have to be perfect, *nobody is*!

Ask for what you want and need. Without this skill, life is a series of disappointments. It is almost impossible to have a good relationship without learning to ask for what you want.

- You can ask for what you want without having to feel guilty about it... and people have the right to tell you, "No," too!

- Your unrealistic thoughts may be scaring you away from asking for what you want; don't let them hold you back!

- You can't be sure people know what you want unless you ask them.

- Practice asking for what you want; it does get easier the more you try!

Chapter **9**

"Just Say No.... Yeah, Right"
(Refusal Skills)

It's 8:00 P.M. — bedtime for two-year-old Tommy. Tommy's mom says, "Pick up your blocks, honey. It's time to go to bed." Tommy shrieks, "No!" and promptly gets a swat on the behind and sent to his room for the night. His mom tells him, "You don't say 'no' to me, young man! You do as you're told!"

Now Tommy turns thirteen, and all of a sudden his mom and dad are after him to "just say no" to sex, drugs, cigarettes and behavior they don't approve of. Tom's had years of practice being polite, trying to do what he's told; but nobody ever told him how to say "no" to very cute and very popular Alyssa, when she says, "You're so funny! I bet you're hilarious when you're high. Come on, let's go smoke a joint. I've got some great pot!"

Alyssa's offer is pretty appealing to Tom for several reasons:

- She's cute and he'd love to spend more time with her.

- His friends would say he's crazy if he didn't go ("Look at her — she's totally hot! You're nuts, man!").

- He'd love to be more popular, and Alyssa could help him.

- She's complimented him — making it harder to refuse her.

Tom doesn't do drugs and doesn't want to start. He says, "Pot might slow down this lightning wit. But if you think I'm funny now, you should see me with a face full of pizza! I'll pay if you want to come with me for some."

Tom's lucky, he's got a good sense of humor and can use it to joke his way out of a situation. He's also offered a better idea, so he may still get together with Alyssa (that is *if* he decides he wants to, and is comfortable spending time with someone who uses drugs).

Saying No

Some people believe the world will come to an end if they say no. Everyone will drop dead. Skyscrapers will disappear into a pile of dust and rubble. Thoughts that stop us from saying no might be: "If I say no: Everyone will hate me. Everyone will leave me. No one will like me. I'm selfish. I won't have any friends. I'll hurt his feelings. People will think I'm rude. It's not nice to say no. People will think I'm mean."

Saying no brings out "catastrophic" thinking — false ideas such as, if you say no to people you will harm them in some terrible fatal way. ("Jeremy will never ask out another girl again if I turn him down — he'll probably get so depressed that he'll end up in a mental hospital.") You fear you may upset them or "permanently scar" them or ruin their lives.

Think about it. None of the above will happen if you say no. People don't really care that much! Imagine someone asking to wear your new jacket and you say no. She says, "Oh!" Even if that person asks why, you can be honest and tell her you've decided not to lend it out. You don't have to apologize or make up excuses. End of subject.

Imagine you ask your friend for a ride to a football game and he says, "Sorry, the car's full already." Do you cry, faint, feel insulted, take it personally? Are you convinced that he doesn't like you anymore? The fact is that the car is full. That's all.

That doesn't mean it's always easy to say no. It can be really tough — especially when you care about the person. "Just saying no" doesn't always come easily. Assertiveness can help a lot.

Here are some assertive ways of saying no that don't sound rude. How about saying, "I'd like to be your project partner, but I already have one. Maybe next time we can work together?" "I can't cut the grass until I finish this, but I'll be sure to do it then." "I really don't have time to do that now. I have to get this done. Can you get someone else to do it for you?"

If you act like it's no big deal to say no, and just stay relaxed, then it doesn't have to be that important for the other person to get you to say "yes." If you're at a party and someone hands you a beer, you can pass it on to the next person, or calmly say "no thanks."

Tom, in our earlier example, used *humor* and *offered a better idea* to avoid doing something he didn't want to do. Both can be good alternatives to straightforward assertiveness, but if cracking jokes isn't easy for you, following these **MAPS** may help:

- *Make an Excuse.* "Nope, I'm driving." Or, "It makes me throw up." (Try to be truthful, though, lies often catch up to you.)
- *Avoid It.* "Hey Chris, let's skip class!" "Oops — gonna be late, we'd better hurry!" (This is only a temporary solution, but can work for a little while.)
- *Pour It On!* "Are you serious?! I can't believe you said that! That stuff'll rot your brain."
- *Switch Directions.* "Wait — I've gotta tell you about what Carlos said to me."

Different situations call for different responses, but using a variation of one of these — or a combination of them — could ease you out of a tight spot.

"Uh Oh, Here Comes Trouble!"

What's the best way to avoid a bad situation? Keep your eyes and ears open, and think ahead — "What's likely to happen here? Do I want to be involved? Is the risk really worth it?"

- If the party's getting a little too wild, you can always leave early.
- If your friends want to drop by Burger World and you've only got fifteen minutes to get home — do you really have time?

Can you make more time by calling ahead and explaining that you'll be late?

- If a casual conversation with friends is turning into a mean gossip session, you can walk away, try to change the subject, or be straightforward: "Jenn's my friend. I'd really like it if you didn't say things about her."

The idea is to sense trouble coming *before* it happens. You don't have to say no if you're not there to be asked!

Peer Pressure

A lot of teenagers think that in order to be popular and have friends, they have to follow along with the crowd. You know all about it: "peer pressure." It can be hard when you really WANT to be a member of a group. You WANT to dress, talk, act and look like your friends. Even if they're doing things that make you uncomfortable — like smoking cigarettes or pot — it's easy to go along to be accepted . . . and to slip into habits that you later regret. Though at times it may seem like it, not everyone is having sex, drinking, and doing drugs; one choice you always have is to look for people who feel the same way *you* do about those things.

Sexual Pressure

Teens are getting involved in sex at an earlier age than ever before. Peer pressure to become sexually active is overwhelming. In order to feel a part of a group or "socially acceptable," some young people are engaging in sex as early as 11, 12, or 13 years old.

When people can't, or won't say no, they sometimes turn to harmful ways of avoiding it. Many young women try to take control of their sexuality by starving themselves into skeletons: *anorexia nervosa*. By staying skinny, they feel safe from male attention. The

"In the Swim"

Julie has been swimming competitively since she was six. She practices an hour or more a day. Getting up early, and going to the pool every day is lonely, hard work. Julie's interest in swimming keeps her from doing a lot of things other teenagers do. Then Julie meets Josh. They really like each other. Josh wants Julie to spend more time with him. His friends smoke, drink, do drugs and stay out late. Julie knows that if she goes along with this crowd she won't achieve her goal of becoming a swimming legend like Michael Phelps. Smoke is bad for her lungs; drinking could hurt her swimming ability. She can't stay out late and still get up at 5:00 A.M. to practice.

What should Julie do? How would you deal with this situation? Here is one assertive way to handle it:

Julie: "I like you a lot, and I love being with you. But swimming means a lot to me too. You know I have to keep competing so I can make the state finals."

Josh: "So what are you saying ... you don't want to go out with me anymore?"

Julie: "No, not that — I *do* want to go out with you, but I'm not going to give up my shot at really going somewhere with my swimming."

Josh: "I'm not asking you to."

Julie: "I know. What I mean is, I can't stay out late more than one night a weekend, and I can't be around your friends when they're smoking — it's bad for my lungs."

Josh: "Yeah ... ?"

Julie: "So I can't go to parties with you, but I still want to go out with you, and maybe you could pick me up after practice sometimes ..."

price they pay is a damaged body. Sometimes they die from malnutrition. Another way young people avoid dealing with sex is to gain so much weight that they no longer feel attractive. Of course they aren't consciously choosing these ways of avoiding sex — they're afraid to deal with it directly.

Young men have pressure on them to be "macho" and have sex. They might want to wait until they're older, but in order to be accepted in their group of friends they feel they either *have to* have sex or lie about it. Both are damaging.

Your sexuality is one of the deepest ways to express caring for yourself and another person — intimate communication on a physical level. It is not something to give away, give in to, or just *try* to see what it's like. It *is* something to consider carefully and make your own choice about.

If you have tried sex, however, that doesn't mean you must continue to be sexually active. You can take back control of your sexual expression. Many people decide they'll only have sex in loving relationships. Without it, sex feels demeaning and unsatisfying to them.

Sexually-transmitted diseases (STDs) are another important factor. You want no part of the AIDS and herpes epidemics. Care in sexual expression has never been more important. If you are choosing to be sexually active, please use disease *and* birth control measures. Most communities have sources where teens can find out more information, such as Planned Parenthood. (See the "Web Resources" section for a list of online resources.)

You have a right to be in charge of your sexuality. Sexual activity often starts at a very early age; many teens haven't had time to develop clear sexual values and to make conscious choices about what they really want. Take time to decide for yourself what's important to you *before* you have sex.

If you feel scared about your sexuality, you have a right to say to yourself, "It's okay for me *not* to have sex until I feel sure that it is right for me." "I don't care what other people think or do, my sexuality is so important to me, I will be my own guide." "I can say no to sexual pressure. My body belongs to me."

When you can give yourself these rights and take charge of your sexuality, you free yourself from the pressures of wanting to be like everyone else. In the end others respect you for standing up for what you believe. Most important of all, you respect yourself!

Drugs

Drugs are pretty easily available to many teens. Smoking, cocaine use, and drinking are often socially acceptable. The long-term effect of drug abuse is a lost life. Each use of mood altering drugs — even cigarettes, caffeine, and alcohol — affects your body negatively. People who use drugs even once take the risk of picking up an expensive habit, an infectious disease (such as AIDS or hepatitis), getting arrested, or endangering themselves or others. Even so-called "natural" substances such as marijuana can harm your lungs and overall health. It's easier *not* to start than to try to stop using; once you're hooked, you've turned control of your life over to the drug.

Many young people live in families with parents who abuse alcohol or other drugs. Their lives can be nightmares of uncertainty and emotional or physical abuse. Unfortunately, those young people are likely to become substance abusers themselves. It's easy for them to say, "Well, my parents have their drugs, and I have mine. They drink, I smoke pot. What's the big deal?" This pattern goes on generation after generation.

The incidence of divorce, accidents, suicides and family violence among substance abusers is astronomical. A 2007 NHTSA (The National Highway Transportation Safety Administration) report showed 13,000 people were killed nationally by drunk drivers with a BAC (Blood Alcohol Concentration) of .08 or higher. Economic losses from substance abuse are estimated at over two hundred billion dollars a year. (This represents both the use of resources to address health and crime consequences as well as loss of productivity to the work force.) Addictions are a leading cause of death and human suffering in the U.S.A. today. These great tragedies, and the loss of happiness, loss of love, and loss of productive lives, are directly related to substance abuse.

If you or someone you know wants help in getting off drugs or wants help coping with someone who is a substance abuser, call Alcoholics Anonymous, Alateen or Al-Anon. They are listed in your phone book. Most cities have hundreds of meetings each week.

Saying No to Real Questions

Sit facing a friend, and practice saying no to the following questions:

"Would you loan me five dollars until Friday?"
"Can I borrow your car?"
"How about skipping school tomorrow?"
"If you love me, you'll prove it."
"Only one puff won't kill you. Go ahead, take it. What's the matter with you? You scared?"
"What are you saving it for? You must be a prude or a lesbian!"
"Everybody smokes. When are you going to at least try it?"
"Come on, it'll look cool if you dye your hair. Don't you want to look awesome? Let me do it for you."
"You ought to try it. It's so fun! You'll never know what you're missing until you do."
"What's the matter with you? You stuck up? It's no big deal. Come on. Don't be a baby."

Saying no gets easier the more you do it.

Saying No Sets You Free

When you are able to say no — whether it's to drugs, sex, favors, or simple requests, you become free. You control your possessions, your time, your body, and make decisions for yourself. It takes practice. Try the activities that follow to get the experience you need.

The Answer Is No!

With a friend, sit facing each other. You start by asking for something such as a favor, a ride, a loan, or something personal, like for her to cut her hair. You ask for just one thing for three full minutes.
Your friend says no in as many different ways as she wishes. Try different approaches. You continue asking for this favor for three minutes — the same favor. Have fun with this practice. Get dramatic; use guilt, threats, and manipulations. After three minutes switch roles. When you each have had a turn, talk about it. How did it feel to ask, to say no? Which was easier? What made the other one harder? Did you feel threatened? Did you ever say just plain "no" without giving reasons or explanations? How do you feel about your partner?

Try it again, this time asking for the same thing for $1/2$ minute each. Does it get easier? Do you think you could use this in real life? Think about a situation where you wanted to say no but didn't. Do you think you could handle it better now?

Ridiculous, but It Works!

With a friend, stand facing each other. Put your hands against your partner's hands, palms touching, and gently push as one of you says "yes" and the other says "no." Sort of a gentle push-of-war. Repeat for a minute and then switch. Now you say "no" and your partner says "yes." Share with your friend what it felt like. Practice this with other people such as another friend, a brother or sister.

"No" Way

When you know what you want to do and how you want to do it, it's a lot easier to say "no" to things that take you away from your goal. You're in charge of your body, your time, your possessions. You make the decisions that control your life.

Saying no gains us time, space and the opportunity to be ourselves and develop our skills and talents:

- The world won't come to an end if you say no. If you are assertive and direct, the problem or question is quickly taken care of. Following the **MAPS** on page 69 may help you respond, too.

- Avoid bad situations by paying attention, thinking ahead, and sensing trouble *before* it happens. Saying no to putting yourself in an *uncomfortable* situation can help prevent you from getting into a *dangerous* one.

- Peer pressure for activities such as sex, drugs, or alcohol use, which don't feel right to you, can be tough to say no to when you want to fit in. It's easier when your friends have similar values and beliefs to yours, and when you allow yourself the right to be in charge of your body and your decisions.

Chapter 10

"C'mon Baby... You Know You Want To!"
(Avoiding Manipulation)

Lynnae and Cole, both high school sophomores, have been dating for two months. One Saturday night on their way to Lynnae's house after the movies, Lynnae says, "Cole, do you like me?"

"That's dumb, you know I do!"

"Yeah, but I mean *really* like me."

"I *really* like you, Lynnae."

"I think I love you, Cole."

Cole smiles, "Who, me?"

"Yeah," Lynnae turns her head away, "I just wish you loved me."

"Why do you think I don't?"

"Then why won't you make love to me?"

"Lynnae, it's just something I want to be really sure about."

"If you loved me you'd want to."

What a classic line! Lynnae's doing her best to manipulate Cole into doing something he doesn't want — or is not ready — to do. He says, "I care enough about you that I don't want us to rush into this — when or if it happens I want it to be special. I want us both to be ready, and I'm not." Cole's honest answer doesn't allow Lynnae much room for more manipulation.

Manipulation is getting people to do what you want without asking directly. When you ask, people have a chance to say no. When you manipulate, few people can avoid it. (Lynnae doesn't say, "I want to have sex with you, Cole." She says, "If you loved me, *you'd* want to.")

We all know how to manipulate. As small babies we earned our living manipulating. If we weren't cute and cuddly, we would have problems getting enough to eat and our diapers changed. We learned to sense our parents' moods. If Dad was grumpy we stayed away. If Mom was happy, we could get anything we wanted by just pointing.

Why does a book on self-esteem have an entire chapter on manipulation? Because communicating in this way can harm self-esteem — whether you are the manipulator, or the one being manipulated. It's not an honest way to communicate, so you may feel guilty and dishonest about using it, or hurt and disappointed when it is used against you. Nobody wins this game.

The Game

It takes two to play the manipulation game. One person *wants* something. The other person *needs* something. Neither party may be aware that the subtle game has started. The manipulator senses what you need and very indirectly offers it to you. Unaware of the game, you feel fortunate to have such a "nice" person interested in you. You're flattered. You sense what the other person wants and you provide it. The two of you have an unspoken contract. You decide, maybe unconsciously, to exchange services. These services can be things like "I'll compliment you and tell you what a wonderful person you are (whether or not I think that's true). In return you'll be my friend and defend me from the Cutthroat gang down the street."

There's nothing wrong with helping someone in return for a favor: "You scratch my back and I'll scratch yours." The difference between true "give and take" and manipulation, however, is that manipulation is not an honest way to get what you want. It can be hurtful, as it often involves using guilt, fear, and criticism to influence people. Manipulation is whenever someone tries to get something from you that you don't want to give, or tries to make you do something you don't want to do.

Champion Manipulators — Families of Alcoholics or Drug Addicts

Families of alcoholics and drug addicts can be skilled manipulators. They often avoid the truth and deny reality, everyone working together to keep from directly dealing with the addict's problem. One person hides the drugs or bottles, another might partially empty them and replace the contents with something else, a third hides the car keys, someone else lets the air out of the tires to keep the addict from driving. This goes on for years with no one discussing the situation. Each is independently trying to manipulate the addict to stop drinking or using. They think they are saving the drinker/user. Unfortunately, children of addicts often grow up, leave home, and either become addicts themselves or marry them — all the while denying there is a problem. Nobody wins this game of denial, the manipulation just continues for another generation.

Any member of an alcoholic's or drug addict's family can choose to seek help since all members of the family are affected by this sickness. There are thousands of treatment centers, hospital treatment programs, and counselors who specialize in helping alcoholics or other addicts and their families. If one member of the family works at getting well, that improves the probability that others will decide to get well too. (See also page 74 for more resources.)

Manipulative Styles

Many manipulation styles are variations of the same type — one in which the manipulator appeals to another person's sense of compassion, guilt, or even fear. Learning to recognize the style a manipulator is using can help you avoid their drama so you won't be pulled into it. Here are some examples which might seem familiar:

The Victim. This person adopts powerlessness and passivity as a way of life. The victim's body language signals the world, "Here I am. Come beat me, kick me, hurt me. I'm available for abuse." Passive doormats manipulate others to take care of them, solve their problems, feel sorry for them, and give them lots of attention. They offer opportunities for caretakers to feel powerful, intelligent, capable and compassionate.

The Depressed. Depressed people, with a little luck, collect Helpers and Rescuers. They choose to give up the joys of life to focus on negatives. Depressed persons see what is bad, ugly, and isn't there, rather than the love, beauty and happiness which are there. The *set up* is to get people to feel sorry for them. The *payoff* is to get others to take care of them. (Depression is a real illness however, and can be treated. See chapter 5 for more information.)

The Blamer. This victim can identify why he is so unhappy. The cause can be a natural event such as the weather ("It must be 'El Niño!'"), or another person's actions. "Look what you did to me" is a favorite lament. "It's all your fault." "Everybody's mean to me." The manipulation is to get other people to take responsibility for the blamer's life and make it up to him. The *set up* is to get people to feel guilty, the *payoff* is release from guilt.

The Button-Pusher. "I will throw you off balance by finding out what really gets to you and using it against you." If you are sensitive about your weight, the button-pusher might make a comment about you being thin or overweight to upset you aren't thinking clearly: "Hey 'Twiggy,' you're not afraid to try this, are you?"

The Hypochondriac. This person chooses sickness to avoid coping with life. As with the other victim styles it limits joy, fun, and happiness. This is a painful way of getting needs met! The *set up* and the *payoff* are the same as for the other examples above; however, the hypochondriac may have more actual physical pain.

The Suicidal. Manipulation can have permanent results: combining depression and blaming, some people attempt suicide to get even or to make those left behind feel guilty, others genuinely don't want to live anymore. However, any person who seems very depressed or talks about suicide should be taken to a mental health center or professional therapist. Don't risk losing a loved one; tell a parent, trusted teacher or counselor if you know someone like this — they need help immediately. Many people go through periods in their lives when they feel depressed enough to attempt suicide. Very often just talking to a counselor helps them overcome their problems, heal quickly, and go on to lead normal lives.

The Rescuer. "I will save you, give you what you need and you will be *mine*. I will earn your love with brave deeds. You will have to be weak and needy. You will let me take care of you. You will feel you owe me for saving you."

The Martyr. "I will work so hard that you will not be able to get along without me. You will *need* me. I will do your homework, cook your meals, and do all the unpleasant jobs. I will work THREE jobs. I will cripple you with my love so that you will not be able to take care of yourself and you will never leave me."

The Salesman. It is this manipulator's job to get you to say "yes." He starts out asking questions that make you agree, "You believe in feeding starving children, right? And you think people should help them?" and keeps that up until you are so used to saying yes that it's nearly impossible to say no! "You'd be willing to give just a few pennies a week, wouldn't you?"

The Enabler. There have been stories in the news about people who are so obese that they can't leave their beds. The quantity of food they consume is enormous. Who's bringing them all that food? Enablers who truly don't mean them harm. An enabler might say, "I love you and I wish you'd diet," but they continue to provide the care which enables the (food) addict to live as he does.

Fairy Tale Roles

We all grew up listening to fairy tales and most of us know them by heart. Though the stories may be old, their morals can still help us today.

Cinderella or Cinderfella. Cinderella was a classic victim-martyr. She was *rescued* by her fairy godmother who gave her what she needed (dress, shoes, coach . . .) so that she could attend the ball. At the ball she met the Prince, and they fell in love. Since *romance* is supposed to heal all problems, the Prince *rescued* Cinderella and they lived happily ever after.

By being sad and helpless, Cinderella attracted rescuers to help her. She was not assertive. If she were assertive she would have found her own clothes and gotten herself to the ball!

Moral: If you are sitting waiting for a prince or princess to rescue you, forget it! *Save yourself.* There are no more fairy godmothers and very few princes. The *only sure way* of being rescued is to make it a "do it yourself" project!

Little Red Riding Hood: The Gotcha Girl. Little Red Riding Hood is a darling child: big eyes, a "good" expression, and *very* innocent. Dancing through the woods carrying a basket of food for grandma, Red looks like a fetching, tasty morsel. The Wolf, seeing the sweet innocence of this delectable child, decides to follow, outsmart and eat Red. Red, however, has a lot of anger that doesn't show. Realizing at last that a Wolf is following, Red devises a plot. The Wolf gets killed.

Moral: Sometimes "sweet and innocent" people lead you through the forest to get you in trouble at Grandmother's house. While setting up Red, the Wolf was beaten at his own game. The Wolf was led to his death by a passive-aggressive Red.

Peter Pan. "Come fly with me! Life is a ball. I will never grow up. Come live in fantasyland with me. We will drink wine, laugh, dance and sing and never pay attention to reality. We will never feel pain, never cry. The car may get smashed, but we won't care. Maybe we can find a Wendy mate to take care of us and clean up our messes. Let's let her be responsible so that we can play."

Moral: Allowing yourself to be manipulated — by wine, drugs, whatever (or *whomever*) — can get you stuck so you never grow up. Better learn how to take care of yourself. Sooner or later you'll have to.

Fairy tales have had a place in many of our lives. Most of us have a favorite. How does yours relate to your beliefs about yourself and the way you live *your* life?

How Do You Know You're Being Manipulated?

Stay in touch with your body and listen to your thoughts. If you pay attention, your body will let you know that things are not right. It could be a queasy feeling or knot in your stomach, or a headache. You may feel uncomfortable, or feel you are being used. As you become sensitive to manipulation, you and your body will get better at recognizing it.

When you are being manipulated you are living someone else's life: going where they want to go and doing what they want to do. You are not following your own values, interests and goals. It doesn't feel good.

Is your manipulator so much smarter than you that she should be running your life for you? Of course not! *Nobody* knows what you want better than you do! It's your life — shouldn't you be in charge of it?

Techniques for Dealing with Manipulation

By knowing yourself and your rights, you can be free from manipulation. However, if you would like to teach a manipulative person how to be more honest, here are some suggestions:

- **Ask a manipulator, "What do you want?"** A dedicated manipulator probably will be deeply offended and go away, or give you a slick answer, "Not a thing." A person who is willing

Set up and keep a log for a week or two. It will help you recognize when others are manipulating you as well as when and how you manipulate. You will discover your vulnerable points. You will begin to see patterns.

When you are in a situation where you are manipulating or being manipulated, write down what the situation is, who you are with, what you want, and what happened.

Here's an example:

Where? School.

Who manipulated whom? Mark manipulated me.

What happened? He asked to borrow five dollars and I loaned it to him.

What was the set up? He had offered me a ride to school because he needed money for gas.

What was the payoff? Maybe I could continue to ride to school with him.

What did I want? I did not want to lend him money.

How did I feel? I felt manipulated.

What I could have done? I could have asked him if he wanted me to pay for the ride to school each day. I could have asked him right out what he wanted in return for the ride. I could have found another way to get to school.

Review your log to see how people get to you by using your needs. Collecting this information will help you understand manipulation, both yours and other people's.

to learn will hesitate and then try to talk about her needs. It may be a struggle. It may go against all previous training. Be patient.

A friend of mine will compliment me profusely before getting around to the favor he needs to ask. I've learned to ask, "Why are you *really* here?" as soon as he starts in. He's gradually learning that I appreciate an honest request much more than false compliments and his style has changed.

- **Communicate honestly using "I language."** Ask the manipulator for more information: "Where will we be going? When? How are we going to get there?" You can state clearly how you feel about the plans and what you want.

  Let's say your mother's birthday is coming up. You have the feeling that she wants something special since she's been hinting around. You might say to her, "Mom, I have a feeling there is something special you would like for your birthday and I'm feeling frustrated that I don't know what it is. Would you be willing to tell me what it is so I can try to get it for you?"

- **Serve as a model.** When you can express your needs and wants clearly, you help others learn to do this too. They'll get used to your straight talk and probably even like it (if you're careful not to be pushy or aggressive!). As you take responsibility for asking for what you want, you win the respect of others so that they want to act like you!

"Don't Call Me Baby!"

Manipulation comes from weakness or fear. It is used by people who are not willing — or don't know how — to be honest with themselves or others. People may manipulate because they feel they can't ask for what they want or need because no one cares enough to give it to them. Manipulation is supposed to be "polite," however, it robs others of choices, and doesn't let them take responsibility for themselves. It can be very frustrating — even to the manipulator: "I keep dropping hints that I want him to take me to the dance, but he just doesn't get it!"

People who choose manipulation seek control in underhanded ways. They play games rather than risk being honest. Learning to be direct allows the manipulative person to gain self-respect.

The manipulative person is highly skilled at reading others. It takes incredible sensitivity to know what others need and to offer it to them in subtle ways. Imagine using this talent to *help* people!

We all can be manipulative in one way or another. It is your choice whether you wish to continue to manipulate. Each time you take the risk of making honest statements to others, you win respect. You may decide to give up your role or "victim" style; you'll find yourself growing in self-respect and liking yourself more. Playing games is wonderful fun when it is open competition. Playing games to get what you want defeats self-respect and robs others of free choice. Honesty really is the best policy.

C'mon baby. You know you want to *avoid manipulation* . . . and now you know how!

Stop Playing the Manipulation Game

- Recognize the manipulative style so it isn't used against you. Don't let the manipulator push your buttons, pull you into the drama, or catch you up in the fairy tale.

- Notice how your body is feeling so you are aware of when you are being manipulated and can better avoid it. Do you feel queasy or tense? What is behind the manipulator's words that is bothering you?

- It takes two people to play the manipulation game. If you refuse to be manipulated by asking for honest communication, then the other person can't "play" you! Say, "Tell me what you really want." Your assertive communication may inspire theirs.

Chapter 11

Not to Decide Is to Decide
(Choices and Decision Making)

We all make hundreds of decisions every day, from what to wear to how to answer questions on a quiz. Most of them we don't really have to think much about, but occasionally there comes a situation where we almost wish we could have someone choose for us. *Almost.* You don't get what you want when you don't decide for yourself — so even when the choice isn't an easy one it's worth giving it your best shot.

There is help, though. Here are some steps that are useful to follow when making a decision:

- What's the problem? (What's the decision to be made?)
- What are the alternatives?
- List the good points for each.
- List the bad points for each.

We'll start with a tough one:

Brittany knows that her friend Callie's dad tends to drink too much, and when he does he gets violent. Callie has come to school with black eyes and bruises before. She still loves her dad, so she tells the teachers that she tripped and fell, or that her horse bucked her off. But she's told Brittany that her dad has beaten her up, and now he's starting on her little brother, Todd. Brittany wants to tell someone who can do something about it, but Callie's made her swear not to. As Brittany thinks about what to do, she might write it down like this:

- *What's the problem?*
  Whether or not to tell an adult about Callie's dad.

- *What are the alternatives?*
  a) Don't tell.
  b) Tell police.
  c) Tell teacher.
  d) Tell my parents.

- *Good points of each alternative:*
  a) Don't tell: Callie won't be mad at me.
  b) Tell police: Callie won't be hurt anymore.
  c) Tell teacher: Same.
  d) Tell my parents: Get help with decision.
                               Callie could be helped.

- *Bad points of each alternative:*
  a) Don't tell: Callie could get seriously hurt.
  b) Tell police: Callie's dad could be arrested.
                          Callie would hate me.
  c) Tell teacher: Same (They're required by law to tell police).
  d) Tell my parents: They might tell police.

Try to find the choice where the good points outweigh the bad. In Brittany's case, that choice is to tell her parents.

Remember that there's a difference between "telling on" someone and telling someone who can help with the problem. If you are "telling" in order to get someone in trouble, then you're not really helping. But if you think that someone might be hurt if you *don't* do something, the best choice is to ask for help.

Here's an easier problem: Your parents are always after you to turn your music down — they hate popular music. You're tired of fighting about it.

- *Problem:* Do I have to give up my music to get along with Mom and Dad?

- *Alternatives:*
    e) Put up with the fighting.
    f) Trade in my CD's for Mozart.
    g) Listen to music at whisper level.
    h) Buy headphones or ear buds.

- *Good points of each alternative:*
    e) Get to listen to my music (for a while).
    f) Mom and Dad would love it.
    g) Parents wouldn't bug me.
    h) Could listen to my music loud. Quit fighting.

- *Bad points of each alternative:*
    e) They've threatened to take my speakers away.
    f) I hate classical music.
    g) Music doesn't sound as good.
    h) I'd have to save money.

Sometimes just writing down the problem and the alternatives will make your choice clear; at others you may need to go to a counselor, friend or parent for more advice. Just remember — the final decision is yours.

More Decision Making Hints

- **Do you have enough information to make a decision?** Let's say you want to go to France to study art. Where are the places to go for information? Do you need to learn French? You could

Get Help When You Need It

We all need help now and then — it's just as important to know when to ask for help with a hard decision as it is to be able to decide for yourself at other times. Think about the people you find easy to talk to, or who've given you good advice. You may want to jot down their names to look at when you really need someone to talk to, or some specific help.

Here are some examples:

> School counselor
>
> Friend
>
> Teacher
>
> Neighbor
>
> Older brother, sister, cousin, etc....
>
> Local family services or counseling center
>
> Hotline (crisis telephone service)
>
> Mom/Dad, Grandma/Grandpa
>
> Minister/Coach/Youth group leader

consult an encyclopedia, a travel agent, or the French consul to find answers. Many people will give you ideas and other names of people who can help you to learn more about how to get to France, where to study and what you'll need in order to get ready.

- **Give yourself time to make a good decision.** Hurrying won't help. Ask people their opinions. Sleep on it. If it's a career choice, explore; interview people in different professions; stay flexible and open. During the summer you can work in a field that interests you. Practical experience in the field will help you decide about whether or not it's right for you.

- **Delay making a decision until you're sure you know what is right for you.** Decisions need to be made with all of you: head, heart, spirit, and emotions. Don't deny the gut-level decision. Don't let your head talk the emotional part of you out of a decision (as long as your choice allows you to stay safe and healthy). Those decisions made deep down in your gut are usually "right." Remember, you can always change your mind.

- **Look at many alternatives.** Don't get trapped into an either/or choice (I'll go to college or become a janitor.) If you relax your body and daydream a little, you may come up with a variety of ways to solve the problem or make the decision. The only limit is your imagination. Knowing alternatives gives you a feeling of being powerful and in charge of your life. The more choices you give yourself, the more freedom you have.

Remember that you are choosing all the parts of your life (education, career, values, relationships, personal "style," ...), and you are free to change any of the parts you don't like.

Of course, there are consequences for your choices. For instance, you decide to stay up to watch the Super Horror Show at 2:00 A.M. You'll be tired the next morning — but the show may be worth it! Or, so that you can save your money until you have enough to go to that favorite band's concert, you can choose not to spend it for snacks, movies or video games — it's your decision!

If you're unhappy, you're choosing to be unhappy. Please don't blame it on others. Abraham Lincoln said, "We are just about as happy as we choose to be." If you work at a job you hate, realize that you choose to work there. Don't complain. Find a better job, create your own job, start your own business. Take responsibility for being where you are, doing what you are doing. If you don't like it, change it if you can. Even if the causes of your unhappiness are significant (serious health problems, unmet physical needs, abusive families), there is help and hope available. Ask your school counselor, a minister, advisor, or someone else you trust for help with your situation. Change *is* possible.

Problem Solving

Most people fear trouble and problems. They get upset when things don't go the way they expect. As things frustrate them, they get angry. It's O.K. to be angry. The extra energy that anger gives us can be useful in correcting what is bothering us. Most people get emotional over life changes, people changes and disappointments. It is important to avoid letting your emotions scare you into making a poor choice, though. If you sense yourself losing control, back off for a while. Hold off on making your decision until you've calmed down. (See chapter 7's discussion on dealing with anger.)

What kinds of things upset you? Can you change them?

Mistakes as Opportunities

Another way to look at problems is as *opportunities*. Watch a tiny baby. The baby learns by testing, tasting, feeling and making mistakes like bumping into things. Often the very best way to learn is to make mistakes.

For instance, if you left your bike outside when you were younger and it was stolen or broken, you may have learned to put your bike away. The lesson probably was terribly painful at the time. But, through this experience you learned that when you leave your possessions outside, they may be lost, stolen or broken. Looking back, you may even be grateful for learning that lesson at a young age.

Where Are You Headed?

As you get older, of course, life's decisions become more complex. Will you work hard enough to make it into college? What career will you go into? Where will you make your home?

Imaging a Problem

If you have a problem, find a room or a quiet place where you won't be disturbed. Close the door. Put on soft music. Get yourself comfortable. Now relax your body. Let the tension gradually run out of your body. Feel it draining out of your joints and filtering out of your fingers and toes. Work at this until you feel like a limp, sleepy, puppy.

Now that you're relaxed, imagine the solution to your problem has already been found. You have a warm feeling all over your body and mind. No need to be upset. Now play with the idea that there are lots of ways of solving the problem.

Think of as many ways as you can. Don't judge them. Go ahead and think of ridiculous solutions like getting on a slow boat to Australia. (I always think of getting on a slow boat to Australia as the first solution to all my problems. It makes me laugh and puts me in the proper mood to solve a problem creatively.)

Stay completely relaxed. Play with the ideas and you will probably come up with a number of ways to solve your problem.

Try to find unusual ways. Imagine what would happen if you did things like talk to the person who is causing the problem. Imagine a calm, reasonable tone to your voice. See yourself presenting strong ideas. See yourself being kind and caring. See a positive result. Imagine the person's response to you. Write down this conversation. Practice it with a friend or family member.

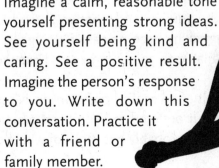

Some people seem always to have known where they were headed. Clear goals can make decisions easier.

If you decide at age ten that you want to be a lawyer, your life is relatively simple. You study political science, language and writing, history and debating (if your school has a team or class). You might study speech, drama and voice training if you're interested in courtroom cases or becoming a legislator. You may decide what college you want to attend and choose to get good grades. You might even win a scholarship. You may work in a law office doing paralegal work on vacations and take the law aptitude exam toward the end of your college career. The progress you make is simple and clear.

But what if you don't know what you want to do with your life? That makes it a lot more difficult to make decisions. Avoiding it doesn't help. Not deciding is making a decision — you're letting others decide for you, or letting life pass you by.

The best approach, if you're not sure, is to take some small risks. Make minor decisions — based on good information — and try them out. (The more information you have about your alternatives, the more freedom you have to make good choices.) If things aren't working, make changes to "fine tune" your direction.

"And the Answer Is..."

It takes effort to explore who you are and to find your own truth. As you are willing to clarify who you are and what you stand for, problem solving and decision making become easier. Being aware of the richness of choices available to you enlarges and expands your life possibilities.

Take advantage of opportunities to make your own decisions. Avoid "I don't care." Express your preferences! You'll get practice in making decisions — and you'll probably get more of what you want from life!

Decision Making Steps:

- Identify the *problem*, the *alternatives*, and the *good and bad points for each*. Find the choice where the good points outweigh the bad.

- Get the *information* you need; give yourself plenty of *time*; use your *head, heart, spirit and emotions*; look at many *alternatives*.

- Look at problems or mistakes as *opportunities*; you can *learn from the experience* and it may even make future decisions easier.

- *Setting clear goals* can make decision making easier; it allows you to take small steps or risks toward your goals and get more information about your alternatives.

Chapter 12

Taking Charge
(Freedom & Responsibility)

Free at last!
Let's say you're eighteen, you're graduating from high school, and you can do whatever you want, right? No more Mom and Dad telling you what to do, where to go, and with whom...finally!

But...wait a minute, that means no more Mom and Dad buying food and clothes, answering the phone when you don't want to talk to that "gross jerk" you just broke up with, Mom's killer lasagna, free rent...

Help!

Okay, maybe you're going off to college, will live in a dorm, eat in the cafeteria, and your parents are paying for the whole ride. Or maybe you've still got several years before you graduate. Whatever your situation, the point is that *you're going to be in charge of the rest of your life!* You'll have to make the decisions — they won't always be easy. But you've read this book. You know how to:

- make a good decision,
- act on it assertively,
- avoid being manipulated,
- ask for what you want,
- handle your anger,

- say no,

- decide what's important to you,

...and you even like yourself a little bit! What's the problem? You're ready for anything, right?

Well, probably not *anything* — life tends to throw surprises at us when we least expect them — but you've learned some good skills and you feel pretty darn *capable*.

Great! That's what self-esteem is all about!

So you won't mind all the new responsibilities that are coming your way. I mean, you've already got *lots* of responsibilities and you handle them with no problem, right?

Right?

Okay, so you forgot to feed the dog that one time, but basically you're...Well, there were the times you hit the alarm's snooze button, slept in, and were going to be late for class, so Dad drove you, and he was late for work...And then you "forgot" to tell your parents about the parent/teacher conference with Ms. Knowitall (and she was *really* mad)...And...

Hmmmm, maybe we'd better work on this a little bit...

How Other People Think You Should Live

The center of your life is you, not another person's needs, wants or desires. This may sound selfish, but if you spend your whole life doing what others want you to do, you'll never get a chance to be productive, creative and independent.

As you grow up, what your parents think of you is very important. How you see yourself comes from what they think of you. You "make your living" by pleasing them. You need them to feed you, to provide clothes, a home and protection. Your parents are probably raising you the way they were raised — with a few improvements they've added to what they learned from *their* parents. They probably act the way they think people *should* act. Your mom might have put clean clothes on you when you were a baby so the neighbors would think she was a good mother. And on it goes.

Don't "Should" on Yourself

Most people are concerned with what other people think. You probably dress, speak, act, work the way you think you "should." When you hear yourself say, "I should (or "have to," "must," "ought to," "better," "got to") however, look out. Ask yourself what *you* want to do. Lots of times when you're using "shoulds" it means you're doing what someone else (parent, friend, teacher neighbor, . . .) wants you to do.

To be in control of your own life, you need to separate out the "shoulds" and "have tos" from the "want tos."

"I don't *have* to study for this test, but I will because I *want* to get a good grade."

You can't live your life the way others want you to because everybody will want you to live it *their* way. You'll feel like a pretzel if you try to please everybody. You'll end up not knowing who you are or what you want.

There are times when it is wise to question authority. In a crowd, anyone with a loud voice can sound like an authority and create panic. Following advice from guidance counselors and parents about your career interests can be good; however, the final decisions need to come from you. Authorities, even parents, cannot know what will make you happy. You must find your own final answers.

Taking Charge

It is important to please yourself, not just with the little things (like buying those $100 running shoes), but to be happy with the direction your life is taking. Your parents probably use the word a lot: *responsibility*. They might use it when they're angry with you: "You can't even remember to take out the trash, and you think you can take responsibility for your own car (horse, motorcycle)?"

"Responsibility" can be a pretty confusing concept. It helps to think of it on four levels:

- *Being responsible* for a specific action means you *caused* it to happen ("Who's responsible for this mess?")

- *Having responsibility* for a specific action means being *obligated* to do it. ("Miguel, you're responsible for taking out the trash every night this week.")

- *Taking responsibility* for an action means you *agree* to do it, and you accept the praise or blame for the result. ("I'll take responsibility for getting the chips and dip for the party.")

- *Being a responsible person* means acting like an *adult*, having goals and initiative, seeing what needs to be done and doing it. ("Jess, it was very responsible of you to call the plumber and get the leak fixed while we were out of town.")

Mom and Dad come home from work to find chocolate chip cookie dough and dirty dishes taking over the kitchen. "Who's responsible for this mess?" they roar at you and your brother. You did it, but you say "Joey did it, Ma." Are you responsible for it? Yes. Are you taking responsibility? No. Are you being a responsible person? No.

Taking responsibility helps you learn to become a more responsible person.

. . . Mowing the lawn because you have to if you want to go to the movies is having responsibility.

... Mowing the lawn without being asked, because you see it needs it, is being a responsible person.

See?

Lots of people hate the idea of taking responsibility for their lives because they are so used to playing the "poor me" game:

"Dad left when I was two years old. Poor me."

"My parents are divorced. Oh, woe is me. I am a helpless victim of fate."

"My father drinks. My life is hopeless."

Sure these are real problems — but they don't have to ruin your life. Everyone has setbacks; overcoming them, and learning from them is what helps us grow and change. Some people don't want to take responsibility because they enjoy blaming others so much. "If only my little brother didn't bother me when I'm trying to study, I could get better grades." "If I'd been born with another leg, I could run twice as fast." It's often easier to blame than to take responsibility, but you're only lying to yourself and others.

No Stop Signs... Speed Limits

Nobody can make your life miserable except you; and you're the only one who can make it terrific, too. We all set our own limits.

If you *believe* you're not going to get that job, fix that car, finish that report ... you very likely won't be able to.

But the opposite is also true; tell yourself that you *can* do it, and you probably will. Before Roger Bannister became the first person to run a mile in less than four minutes in 1954, everyone said that it was physically impossible for that limit to be broken — humans simply could not run that fast. But Bannister didn't set limits on himself — he did his best, and his best broke the "impossible" limit. When others found out it *could* be done, they did it too — *because they now believed it was possible.*

Visualization

- Relax

- Close your eyes

- See yourself doing well at ... taking an exam ... asking someone out ... playing a concerto perfectly ... driving a manual transmission (stick shift) car ...

When you accept responsibility for your life, you've got to accept that possibilities and opportunities are available to you. If you don't, you set your limits before even starting.

Taking Charge of Your Life

Being responsible doesn't have to be boring — it just means that you have more control over your life, and you can determine your own attitude, goals and limits. If you set a course and plan to follow it, no one can stop you but you. You're powerful.

You become powerful when you take charge and responsibility for all of your life. That means when you make a mistake, you don't blame someone else. You learn from making the mistake. You become wiser, more experienced and more effective by using the mistake as a lesson. You allow yourself to have opinions, to have rights, and to speak up when necessary. Each time you take the risk of using your power, you learn it works and that you CAN make a difference!

Your power allows you to make your life whatever you want it to be. Knowing your likes and dislikes, and expressing them if necessary, helps you to have the kind of life you want. You don't need to wait for someone to offer you what you want. You are free to ask for it, or simply get it for yourself. You are in charge of your life and are only limited by the size of your dream. With the awareness of your power, your dream can become reality.

Personal power is tremendously effective if you are willing to use it. One letter to the proper authority can profoundly effect social, political and economic institutions. A phone call can create change. You have the power to correct wrongs, to influence the thinking of others, and to offer solutions to problems.

You Have the Power

There is power and self-esteem inside of you. You can use it to take charge of your life or you can give it away. Most people prefer to deal with you as an equal. They don't *want* you to give them your power and they don't want you to take their power away, either.

You can use your power to change your life — or the world — if you choose. You can be a positive force for change and improvement. You can work toward equality and to correct wrongs.

You — with help from your self-esteem — can make a difference.

It's Possible

- You can't live your life trying to please everybody; it's simply not possible to do it. You'll be happier and more productive if you simply take responsibility for your own life and your own happiness.

- We all set our own limits on our lives. If you believe something is possible, you may be able to achieve it... but if you believe you can't, you won't. *Believe you can!*

Selected Readings

Books for Teens

Abuse:

How Long Does it Hurt: A Guide to Recovering from Incest and Sexual Abuse for Teenagers, Their Friends, and Their Families, Cynthia L. Mather and Kristina E. Debye, Jossey-Bass, San Francisco, CA, 2004.

Invisible Girls: The Truth About Sexual Abuse — A Book for Teen Girls, Young Women, and Everyone Who Cares About Them, Patti Feuereisen and Caroline Pincus, Seal Press, Emeryville, CA, 2005.

Strong at the Heart: How It Feels to Heal from Sexual Abuse, Carolyn Lehman, Farrar, Straus and Giroux, New York, NY, 2005.

The Me Nobody Knows: A Guide for Teen Survivors, Barbara Bean and Shari Bennett, Jossey-Bass, San Francisco, CA, 1997.

When Something Feels Wrong: A Survival Guide About Abuse for Young People, Deanna S. Pledge, Free Spirit Publishing, Minneapolis, MN, 2002.

Anger Management:

Hot Stones and Funny Bones: Teens Helping Teens Cope with Stress and Anger, Brian Seaward and Linda Bartlett, HCI Teens, Deerfield Beach, FL, 2002.

Mad: How to Deal with Your Anger and Get Respect, James J. Crist, Free Spirit Publishing, Minneapolis, MN, 2007.

Assertiveness:

How to Say No and Keep Your Friends, Sharon Scott, HRD Press, Amherst, MA, 1997.

Body Image/Eating Disorders:

Dying to Be Thin: Understanding and Defeating Anorexia Nervosa and Bulimia — A Practical, Lifesaving Guide, Ira M. Sacker and Marc A. Zimmer, Grand Central Publishing, New York, NY, 2001.

No Body's Perfect: Stories by Teens about Body Image, Self-acceptance, and the Search for Identity, Kimberly Kirberger, Scholastic, New York, NY, 2003.

Bullying:

The Courage To Be Yourself: True Stories by Teens About Cliques, Conflicts, and Overcoming Peer Pressure, Al Desetta, Free Spirit Publishing, Minneapolis, MN, 2005.

Odd Girl Speaks Out: Girls Write About Bullies, Cliques, Popularity, and Jealousy, Rachel Simmons, Harvest Books, San Diego, CA, 2004.

Depression:

Beating Depression: Teens Find Light at the End of the Tunnel, Faye Zucker and Joan E. Huebl, Scholastic, New York, NY, 2007.

When Nothing Matters Anymore: A Survival Guide for Depressed Teens, Bev Cobain, Free Spirit Publishing, Minneapolis, MN, 2007.

Disabilities:

Different But Equal: Teens Write About Disabilities, Youth Communication, New York, NY, 2005.

Easy for You to Say: Q & A's For Teens Living With Chronic Illness or Disability, Miriam Kaufman, Firefly Books, Buffalo, NY, 2005.

Divorce:

The Divorce Helpbook for Teens, Cynthia MacGregor, Impact Publishers, Atascadero, CA, 2004.

Jigsaw Puzzle Family: The Stepkids' Guide to Fitting It Together, Cynthia MacGregor, Impact Publishers, Atascadero, CA, 2005.

Surviving Divorce: Teens Talk About What Hurts and What Helps (Choices), Trudi Strain Trueit, Scholastic, New York, NY, 2007.

Drug and Alcohol Abuse:

Drugs Explained: The Real Deal on Alcohol, Pot, Ecstasy, and More (A Sunscreen Book), Pierre Mezinski, Melissa Daly, and Francoise Jaud, Harry N. Abrams, New York, NY, 2004.

When Parents Have Problems — A Book for Teens and Older Children with an Abusive, Alcoholic, or Mentally Ill Parent, Susan B. Miller, Charles C. Thomas Publisher, Springfield, IL, 1995.

Wise Highs: How to Thrill, Chill, & Get Away from it All Without Alcohol or Other Drugs, Alex J. Packer, Free Spirit Publishing, Minneapolis, MN, 2006.

Emotional Health/Feelings:

Fighting Invisible Tigers: A Stress Management Guide for Teens, Earl Hipp, Free Spirit Publishing, Minneapolis, MN, 2008.

Life Lists for Teens: Tips, Steps, Hints, and How-Tos for Growing Up, Getting Along, Learning, and Having Fun, Pamela Espeland, Free Spirit Publishing, Minneapolis, MN, 2003.

The Struggle to Be Strong: True Stories by Teens About Overcoming Tough Times, Al Desetta and Sybil Wolin, Editors, Free Spirit Publishing, Minneapolis, MN, 2000.

Too Stressed To Think?: A Teen Guide to Staying Sane When Life Makes You Crazy, Annie Fox and Ruth Kirschner, Free Spirit Publishing, Minneapolis, MN, 2005.

What Teens Need to Succeed: Proven, Practical Ways to Shape Your Own Future, Peter L. Benson, Judy Galbraith and Pamela Espeland, Free Spirit Publishing, Minneapolis, MN, 1998.

Friendship/Relationships:

The How Rude! Handbook of Friendship & Dating Manners for Teens: Surviving the Social Scene, Alex J. Packer, Free Spirit Publishing, Minneapolis, MN, 2004.

The Teen Survival Guide to Dating & Relating: Real-World Advice on Guys, Girls, Growing Up, and Getting Along, Annie Fox and Elizabeth Verdick, Free Spirit Publishing, Minneapolis, MN, 2005.

Girl Stuff:

Dealing with the Stuff That Makes Life Tough: The 10 Things That Stress Teen Girls Out and How To Cope with Them, Jill Zimmerman, McGraw-Hill, New York, NY, 2004.

Girlsource: A Book by and for Young Women About Relationships, Rights, Futures, Bodies, Minds, and Souls, A Girlsource Production, Ten Speed Press, Berkeley, CA, 2003. (for older teens)

Real Girl Real World: A Guide to Finding Your True Self, Heather M. Gray and Samantha Phillips, Seal Press, Emeryville, CA, 2005.

Respect: A Girl's Guide to Getting Respect & Dealing When Your Line is Crossed, Courtney Macavinta and Andrea Vander Pluym, Free Spirit Publishing, Minneapolis, MN, 2005.

Guy Stuff:

100 Things Guys Need to Know, Bill Zimmerman, Free Spirit Publishing, Minneapolis, MN, 2005. (for younger teens)

The Guy Book: An Owner's Manual, Mavis Jukes, Crown Books for Young Readers, New York, NY, 2002.

Our Boys Speak: Adolescent Boys Write About Their Inner Lives, John Nikkah, St. Martin's Griffin, New York, NY, 2000.

The Teenage Guy's Survival Guide: The Real Deal on Girls, Growing Up and Other Guy Stuff, Jeremy Daldry, Little Brown Young Readers, New York, NY, 1999.

Religion/Spirituality:

Teen Spirit: One World, Many Paths, by Paul Raushenbush, HCI Teens, Deerfield Beach, FL, 2004.

What Do You Stand For? For Teens: A Guide to Building Character, Barbara A. Lewis and Pamela Espeland, Free Spirit Publishing, Minneapolis, MN, 2005.

Self-Growth:

The 7 Habits of Highly Effective Teens, Sean Covey, Fireside, New York, NY, 1998.

What Color Is Your Parachute for Teens: Discovering Yourself, Defining Your Future, Richard N. Bolles, Carol Christen, Jean M. Blomquist, Ten Speed Press, Berkeley, CA, 2006.

Sexuality:

Changing Bodies, Changing Lives: A Book for Teens on Sex and Relationships (3rd Edition), Ruth Bell, Three Rivers Press, New York, NY, 1998.

S.E.X.: The All-You-Need-To-Know Progressive Sexuality Guide to Get You through High School and College, Heather Corinna, Da Capo Press, Cambridge, MA, 2007. (for older teens)

The Teen Survival Guide to Dating & Relating: Real-World Advice on Guys, Girls, Growing Up, and Getting Along, Annie Fox and Elizabeth Verdick, Free Spirit Publishing, Minneapolis, MN, 2005.

(See also "Girls Stuff" and "Boys Stuff" resources for more on sex.)

Suicide:

The Power to Prevent Suicide: A Guide for Teens Helping Teens, Richard E. Nelson and Judith C. Galas, foreword by Bev Cobain, Free Spirit Publishing, Minneapolis, MN, 2006.

When Nothing Matters Anymore: A Survival Guide for Depressed Teens, Bev Cobain, Free Spirit Publishing, Minneapolis, MN, 2007.

Violence:

I Wrote On All Four Walls: Teens Speak Out Against Violence, Fran Fearnley, Annick Press, Buffalo, NY, 2004.

Safe Teen: Powerful Alternatives to Violence, Anita Roberts, Raincoast Books, Vancouver, Canada 2002.

Books for Parents and Teachers

Abuse:

How Long Does it Hurt: A Guide to Recovering from Incest and Sexual Abuse for Teenagers, Their Friends, and Their Families, Cynthia L. Mather and Kristina E. Debye, Jossey-Bass, San Francisco, 2004.

Invisible Girls: The Truth About Sexual Abuse — A Book for Teen Girls, Young Women, and Everyone Who Cares About Them, Patti Feuereisen and Caroline Pincus, Seal Press, Emeryville, CA, 2005.

Anger Management:

Anger Management for Everyone, Raymond Chip Tafrate and Howard Kassinove, Impact Publishers, Atascadero, CA, 2009.

Calming the Family Storm: Anger Management for Moms, Dads, and All the Kids, Gary D. McKay and Steven A. Maybell, Impact Publishers, Atascadero, CA, 2004.

Healthy Anger: How to Help Children and Teens Manage Their Anger, Bernard Golden, Oxford University Press, New York, NY, 2006.

Body Image/Eating Disorders:

Help Your Teenager Beat an Eating Disorder, James Lock and Daniel le Grange, The Guilford Press, New York, NY, 2005.

"I'm...Like...SO Fat!": Helping Teens Make Healthy Choices about Eating and Exercise in a Weight-Obsessed World, Dianne Neumark-Sztainer, The Guilford Press, New York, NY, 2005.

Surviving an Eating Disorder (3rd Edition): Strategies for Family and Friends, Michele Siegel, Judith Brisman and Margot Weinshel, Harper Paperbacks, New York, NY, 2009.

When Your Child Has an Eating Disorder: A Step-By-Step Workbook for Parents and Other Caregivers, Abigail H. Natenshon, Jossey-Bass, San Francisco, 1999.

Bullying:

And Words Can Hurt Forever: How to Protect Adolescents from Bullying, Harassment, and Emotional Violence, James Garbarino and Ellen de Lara, Free Press, New York, NY, 2003.

The Bully, the Bullied, and the Bystander: From Preschool to High School — How Parents and Teachers Can Help Break the Cycle of Violence, Barbara Coloroso, HarperCollins, New York, NY, 2004.

Odd Girl Out: The Hidden Culture of Aggression in Girls, Rachel Simmons, Harvest Books, San Diego, CA, 2003.

Depression:

Adolescent Depression: A Guide for Parents, Francis Mark Mondimore, John Hopkins University Press, Baltimore, MD, 2002.

The Disappearing Girl: Learning the Language of Teenage Depression, Lisa Machoian, Plume, New York, NY, 2006.

Understanding Teenage Depression: A Guide to Diagnosis, Treatment, and Management, Maureen Empfield and Nicholas Bakalar, Henry Holt, New York, NY, 2001.

Disabilities:

Breakthrough Parenting for Children with Special Needs: Raising the Bar of Expectations, Judy Winter, Jossey-Bass, San Francisco, CA, 2006.

Reflections from a Different Journey: What Adults with Disabilities Wish All Parents Knew, Stanley Klein and John Kemp, McGraw-Hill, New York, NY, 2004.

Divorce:

Parenting After Divorce: Resolving Conflicts and Meeting Your Children's Needs (2nd Edition), Philip M. Stahl, Impact Publishers, Atascadero, CA, 2007.

Rebuilding: When Your Relationship Ends (3rd Edition), Bruce Fisher and Robert Alberti, Impact Publishers, Atascadero, CA, 2006.

Drug and Alcohol Abuse:

Choices and Consequences: What to Do When a Teenager Uses Alcohol/Drugs, Dick Schaefer, Hazelden, Center City, MN, 1998.

Just Say Know: Talking with Kids About Drugs and Alcohol, Cynthia Kuhn, Scott Swartzwelder, and Wilkie Wilson, W.W. Norton & Co., New York, NY, 2002.

Saying No is Not Enough: Helping Your Kids Make Wise Decisions About Alcohol, Tobacco, and Other Drugs — A Guide for Parents of Children Ages 3 Through 19, Robert Schwebel, Newmarket Press, New York, NY, 1999.

Emotional Health/Feelings:

7 Things Your Teenager Won't Tell You: And How to Talk About Them Anyway, Jenifer Zippincott and Robin M. Deutsch, Ballantine Books, New York, NY, 2005.

10 Best Gifts for Your Teen: Raising Teens with Love and Understanding, Patt and Steve Saso, Sorin Books, Notre Dame, IN, 1999.

Staying Connected to Your Teenager: How to Keep Them Talking to You and How to Hear What They're Really Saying, Michael Riera, Da Capo Press, Cambridge, MA, 2003.

Friendship/Relationships:

How to Talk With Teens About Love, Relationships, & S-E-X: A Guide for Parents, Amy G. Miron and Charles D. Miron, Free Spirit Publishing, Minneapolis, MN, 2002.

What Parents Need to Know About Dating Violence, Barrie Levy and Patricia Occhiuzzo Giggans, Seal Press, Oakland, CA, 1995.

Parenting Teenage Boys:

Raising Cain: Protecting the Emotional Life of Boys, Dan Kindlon and Michael
    Thompson, Ballantine Books, New York, NY, 2000.
Real Boys: Rescuing Our Sons from the Myths of Boyhood, William Pollack and Mary
    Pipher, Owl Books, New York, NY, 1999.

Parenting Teenage Girls:

The Disappearing Girl: Learning the Language of Teenage Depression, Lisa Machoian,
    Plume, New York, NY, 2006.
Reviving Ophelia: Saving the Selves of Adolescent Girls, Mary Pipher, Riverhead, New
    York, NY, 2005.

Sexuality:

*Always My Child: A Parent's Guide to Understanding Your Gay, Lesbian, Bisexual,
    Transgendered or Questioning Son or Daughter*, Kevin Jennings and Pat Shapiro,
    Fireside, New York, NY, 2002.
*Everything You Never Wanted Your Kids to Know About Sex (But Were Afraid They'd Ask):
    The Secrets to Surviving You Child's Sexual Development from Birth to Teens*, Justin
    Richardson and Mark A. Schuster, Three Rivers Press, New York, NY, 2004.

Suicide:

(See "Depression")

Violence:

Protecting the Gift: Keeping Children and Teenagers Safe (and Parents Sane), Gavin De
    Becker, Dell, New York, NY, 2000.

Web Resources
(and Hotlines)

Abuse:
ChildHelp USA — Assists children or teens in crisis whether it be running away, physical abuse, sexual abuse, or other problems. ChildHelp also runs a 24-hour hotline at 1-800-4-A-CHILD. www.childhelpusa.org

RAINN (The Rape, Abuse & Incest National Network) — The nation's largest anti-sexual assault organization. RAINN operates the national Sexual Assault Hotline at 1-800-656-HOPE (4673). RAINN carries out programs to prevent sexual assault, help victims, and ensure that rapists are brought to justice. www.rainn.org

Body Image/Eating Disorders:
National Eating Disorders Association — Information about eating disorders, how to develop healthy eating habits. NEDA also runs a National Toll-Free Information and Referral Helpline: 1-800-931-2237. www.nationaleatingdisorders.org

Overeaters Anonymous — A 12-step program for compulsive overeaters, information, resources, how to find a meeting nearby. www.oa.org

Bullying:
Stop Bullying Now — Information, prevention, tips, and games. www.stopbullyingnow.hrsa.gov

Stop Cyberbullying — Information about preventing and dealing with cyberbullying. www.stopcyberbullying.org

Crisis:
Boystown — This famous organization cares for troubled youth and families in crisis. Hotline 1-800-448-3000 (National Teen Emergency Hotline) open 24 hours/day. Kids can call about any kind of problem they're having. www.boystown.org

Depression:
Depressed Teens — Resources for parents and teens on depression, award-winning video, podcast, articles, FAQ's, etc. www.depressedteens.com

Disabilities:
Disability Info — Guide for Americans with disabilities, with information on teens and youth. Addresses health, legal rights, employment, education, and more. www.disabilityinfo.gov

Drug and Alcohol Abuse:

Al-Anon/Alateen — Support group for teens who are affected by another's drinking. www.al-anon.org/alateen.html

Check Yourself — Info on drugs and alcohol, stories, quizzes, information on drugs and videos. Also has tools to assess whether you have a drug problem. www.checkyourself.com

NIDA for Teens — Information for teens about drugs and their effect on the body by the National Institute on Drug Abuse. www.teens.drugabuse.gov

Emotional Health/Feelings:

Cope Care Deal — General self-help information with specifics about different mental health disorders. Site geared towards teens. www.copecaredeal.org

TeensHealth — Covers topics from body issues, to dealing with bullying, sexual health, more. www.kidshealth.org/teen

Teen Growth — Information and resources for teens, including emotional health, sexuality, family, school and more. Interactive with Q&A's and overviewed by pediatricians for medical accuracy. www.teengrowth.com

Friendship/Relationships:

Teen Relationships — Information about abusive relationships with a quiz to see if your relationship is healthy. www.teenrelationships.org

See "Sexuality" resources for more on relationships.

Sexuality:

PFLAG (Parents, Families and Friends of Lesbian and Gays) — Click on "Get Support" to find help and advice for yourself, or for a friend or relative. www.pflag.org

Sex, Etc. — Teen-created website, with videos, comics, and Q&A's. Thorough treatment of a wide variety of sexual topics. www.sexetc.rutgers.edu/index.php

Teenwire — Sexuality and relationship information from Planned Parenthood. Games, movies and animation, radio, diagrams, quizzes, and dictionary. www.teenwire.com

The Trevor Project — National toll-free helpline for youth questioning their sexuality, in crisis, or considering suicide. With links to resources in your area. Helpline: 1-866-4-U-TREVOR (488-7386). www.thetrevorproject.org

Suicide Prevention:

National Suicide Hotline: 1-800-SUICIDE (784-2433).

The Trevor Project — (*See above.*)

Yellow Ribbon Suicide Prevention Program — Light for Life International is a tax-exempt membership organization which offers suicide prevention strategies and advice. Click on "For Teens" for information on what to do if someone asks you for help, coping strategies, and positive messages written by teens to teens. Hotline: 1-800-273-8255. www.yellowribbon.org

Violence:

National Youth Violence Prevention Resource Center — Violence facts and resources, including info on bullying, aggression, hate crimes, gangs, suicide, and dating violence. National Toll Free Hotline: 1-866-723-3968. www.safeyouth.org

Index

More Books With IMPACT

Body, Mind and Spirit:
Vitamins for Your Whole Health
Gary D. McKay, Ph.D., Erik Mansager, Ph.D., Wayne Peate, M.D.
Softcover: $19.95   320 pages   ISBN: 978-1-886230-81-1
Find out how your mind affects your physical and spiritual
health and how to take care of your mind. Shows what impact
your beliefs about the meaning of life have on body and mind
and how to nurture your spirituality. Discover techniques to help
you manage many challenging life issues.

Luck Is No Accident
Making the Most of Happenstance in Your Life and Career
John D. Krumboltz, Ph.D., Al S Levin, Ed.D.
Softcover: $16.95   168 pages   ISBN: 978-1-886230-53-8
Encourages readers to create their own unplanned events, to
anticipate changing their plans frequently, to take advantage of
chance events when they happen, and to make the most of what
life offers. The book has a friendly, easy style about it, and it is
packed with personal stories that really bring the ideas into focus.

John D. Krumboltz, Ph.D.
Al S. Levin, Ed.D.

Your Perfect Right
**Assertiveness and Equality in Your Life and Relationships
(Ninth Edition)**
Robert E. Alberti, Ph.D. and Michael L. Emmons, Ph.D.
Softcover: $17.95   256 pages   ISBN: 978-1-886230-85-9
Hardcover: $24.95   256 pages   ISBN: 978-1-886230-86-6
The assertiveness book most recommended by
psychologists — fifth most recommended among all self-help
books! Helps readers step-by-step to develop more effective
self-expression.

Impact Publishers®

POST OFFICE BOX 6016 • ATASCADERO, CALIFORNIA 93423-6016
Ask your local or online bookseller, or call 1-800-246-7228 to order direct.
Prices effective January 2010, and subject to change without notice.
Free catalog of self-help and professional resources: visit www.impactpublishers.com

Since 1970 — Psychology you can use, from professionals you can trust.